The Daily Telegraph

TAX GUIDE 1998

PREPARED BY

David B. Genders, F.C.A.

A partner of Sayers Butterworth, Chartered Accountants

HarperCollins*Publishers*

HarperCollins Publishers
P.O. Box, Glasgow G4 0NB

First published as The Daily Telegraph Guide
to Income Tax 1974
22nd edition, completely revised 1998.

© Daily Telegraph 1974, 1998

ISBN 0 00 472136 5

Every effort has been made to provide an
up-to-date text but the publishers cannot accept
any liability for errors, omissions or changes in
detail or for any consequences arising from the
use of information contained herein.

Please note that no reference is intended
to actual individuals.

ACKNOWLEDGMENT

The Inland Revenue forms reproduced in this
book are Crown copyright and are reproduced
with the permission of the Controller of Her
Majesty's Stationery Office.

Typeset by Davidson Pre-Press, Glasgow, G3
Printed in Great Britain by Caledonian International
Book Manufacturing, Glasgow, G64

CONTENTS

Introduction   **vi**

1   The Main Features of Self-Assessment   **1**
Who does it affect? What it means for employees, What it means
for the self-employed, Completion of Returns, Filing dates,
Enquiries, Penalties for late Returns, Tax payments, Penalties and
interest – late payment of tax, Records, A résumé of important dates

2   You and the Inland Revenue   **6**
Tax Offices, The Collector of Taxes, Communicating with
the Inland Revenue, Determinations, Enquiries, Assessments
and appeals, The Taxpayer's Charter, Complaints,
Changes in legislation, Income Tax rates for 1997/98

3   Personal Allowances and Reliefs   **12**
Personal allowance, Married couple's allowance, Age allowances,
Additional personal allowance, Widow's bereavement allowance,
Blind person's relief, Transfer of allowances, Relief on life
assurance premiums

4   Interest Payments and Other Outgoings   **21**
Your own home, Home annuity loans, A home for a dependent
relative, Let property, Business loans, Charitable deeds of covenant,
Gift Aid, Payroll deduction scheme, Private medical insurance,
Vocational training

5   Earnings from Employment   **28**
Code numbers, Forms P60, Changing your job, Expenses,
Employee share ownership, Profit-related pay, Payments on
termination of employment

6   Value Added Tax   **42**
Rates of tax, Registration, Records and accounting, Input tax,
Motor cars and fuel, Special schemes for retailers, Second-hand
goods schemes, Helpful schemes for smaller businesses, Bad debts,
Partial exemption, Routine control by the LVO, Penalties,
surcharges and interest, Supplies to/from EU countries, Appeals,
Complaints

7   The Self-Employed   **51**
Records, Accounts, Standard accounting information,
Adjustment of profits, The current-year basis of taxation,
Post-cessation expenses, Capital allowances, Losses,
The Enterprise Allowance, Business Economic Notes,
Special situations

8   National Insurance Contributions, State Social Security and Insured Benefits   **63**
National Insurance Contributions, State Retirement Pensions,
Social Security Benefits, Insured benefits

9 Personal Pensions   **69**

Eligible individuals, Benefits on retirement, Deferred annuities, Tax relief on premiums, Retirement annuities, Waiver of premium benefits, Personal pension planning

10 Investment Income   **76**

Tax-free income, Rental income, Rent-a-Room, Dividends and interest, Accrued income, Offshore funds, Overseas investment income, Non-qualifying life policies, Tax-Exempt Special Savings Accounts, Personal Equity Plans, Friendly Societies, Enterprise Investment Scheme, Venture Capital Trusts, Joint income

11 The Family Unit   **88**

Marriage, Children, Separation and divorce, Old age, Death

12 The Overseas Element   **94**

Domicile, Residence and ordinary residence, Working abroad – long absences, Working abroad – shorter absences, Working abroad – expenses, Leaving the UK permanently, Calculating annual average visits, Allowances for non-UK residents, Income from UK property, Double taxation relief, Taking up UK residence

13 Capital Gains Tax   **100**

Rate of tax, Husband and wife, Losses, The computation of gains, The indexation allowance, Assets owned on 31 March 1982, Quoted stocks and shares, Unquoted investments, Assets held on 6 April 1965, Valuations, Your private residence, A second home, Chattels, Wasting assets, Part disposals, Business assets, Reinvestment relief, Enterprise Investment Scheme, Venture Capital Trusts, Gifts, Deferred gains on business assets and gifts, Inheritances

14 Completing the Return and Calculating your Tax   **117**

Keeping proper records, Completing the Return, Calculating your tax, What the Inland Revenue does

15 Tax Payments, Interest, Surcharges and Penalties   **138**

Tax payments, Statements of account, Interest, Surcharges, Penalties

16 Elections and Claims – Time Limits   **143**

17 Inheritance Tax   **147**

Potentially exempt transfers, Gifts with reservation, Lifetime gifts, Exemptions, Business property, Agricultural property, Trusts, Rates of tax, Sales at a loss, Payment of tax, Legacies, Intestacy

18 Tax Saving Hints   **154**

Self-Assessment, Allowances and reliefs, Company car benefits, Value Added Tax, Sole traders, Pensions, Tax-favoured investments, Capital Gains, Miscellaneous, Inheritance Tax

Tables   161

1   Inland Revenue explanatory booklets
2   Flat-rate allowances for special clothing and the upkeep of tools
     – 1997/98
3   VAT notices and leaflets
4   Business Economic Notes
5   Rates of National Insurance Contributions for 1997/98
6   DSS explanatory pamphlets
7   Social Security benefits
8   Main Social Security benefits for 1997/98
9   Scope of Liability to income tax of earnings
10   Capital Gains Tax – The Indexation Allowance

1998 Budget Measures   177

INTRODUCTION

The 1996/97 tax year, from 6 April 1996 to 5 April 1997, heralded the most fundamental reform for over 50 years to the system of personal taxation in the UK. Under the banner of 'Self-Assessment' millions of taxpayers now have primary responsibility for working out their own tax bills. The second of the new-style Tax Returns and schedules will be sent out in April 1998 — at about the time this book is published.

What really happened? Firstly, the assessing and tax collecting activities of the Inland Revenue Departments have largely been transferred to taxpayers. Taxpayers must now

- ensure that their new-style Tax Returns are filed with the Inland Revenue by strict deadlines;

- compute their own tax liability (or submit the Return earlier to allow the Inland Revenue to calculate the tax for them);

- make any tax payment due by the stipulated dates.

Secondly, the introduction of 'Self-Assessment' brought with it an entirely new and different regime of interest, surcharges and penalties as well as

- new rules for the keeping of proper records;

- the introduction of a new enquiry regime which allows random selection of cases for enquiry.

This edition of the Guide is intended primarily to deal with the tax system for 1997/98 — the second year of 'Self-Assessment'. The Guide covers not only Income Tax but also Capital Gains Tax, Value Added Tax and Inheritance Tax. The changes in legislation brought about by the 1997 Finance Acts are incorporated within this revised edition. The major proposals on taxation announced by the Chancellor in his Budget this March, which do not come into operation until after 5 April 1998, are set out in the supplement at the end of the book.

The Guide has been written to assist you in understanding the workings of our tax system and to enable you to look after your tax affairs efficiently and with the minimum of difficulty. Understandably you are probably also looking for ways to manage your affairs so you pay less tax. There is no easy way to reduce your annual tax bill. Many of the opportunities to save tax depend upon rearranging your affairs or making timely elections. Nevertheless, I hope that the various tax-saving hints mentioned throughout the Guide will help you pinpoint opportunities to save tax one way or another.

1

THE MAIN FEATURES OF SELF-ASSESSMENT

Self-Assessment is a major change to the tax system intended to simplify the tax rules for all individuals who have to complete a Tax Return. The new regime is built round the Tax Return rather than, as previously, by assessments raised by the Inland Revenue. It gives individuals more responsibility for, and control over, their tax affairs.

Who does it affect?
Everyone who has to complete a Tax Return. That means mainly:

- employees who pay tax at the higher rate;

- other employees, and pensioners, with more complicated tax affairs;

- company directors;

- the self-employed;

- business partners.

If you do not have to fill in a Tax Return there is really no change to the way you pay tax. The Pay-As-You-Earn (PAYE) system, and other arrangements for deducting tax at source, continue unchanged.

If you have income or gains to report, which may give rise to a tax liability, and you don't receive a Tax Return, you have six months after the end of the tax year to tell the Inland Revenue and request a Return to fill in.

What it means for employees
In practice the majority of employees do not normally need to submit Tax Returns. Their only source of income is from their employment and tax is deducted at source under PAYE. The PAYE system works in such a way that the correct amount of tax is deducted for the year. However, whilst the PAYE system continues, Self-Assessment nonetheless affects all employees as there is now a legal requirement for all individuals to keep records of their income, expenses and capital gains.

What it means for the self-employed

Under Self-Assessment the self-employed (including partners) are taxed on the profits of their business for the accounting period ending in the tax year. Therefore, for example, if you are in business and make up your accounts to 30 June each year the profit that you make for the year to 30 June 1997 will have to be declared in your Tax Return for the year to 5 April 1998.

Completion of Returns

Tax Returns now require actual figures to be inserted. 'To Be Advised' or 'Per P11D' no longer suffices! Incomplete Returns count as late Returns.

If a Return cannot be fully finished on time because some figures cannot be ascertained the Return should still be submitted by the filing date. It should include an estimate for the unknown information and that fact should be made clear on the Return.

Filing dates

The latest filing dates for Returns are:

30 September   – when you want the Inland Revenue to calculate your
(following the end   tax;
of the tax year)   and for employees:

– where any PAYE underpayments up to £1,000 are to be included in next year's coding;

31 January   – if you calculate your own tax.

You should receive your Tax Return around the beginning of April each year – the start of the tax year. If the Return is issued to you late you will always have three months after the date of issue to submit the Return (or two months if you want the Inland Revenue to calculate your tax bill).

Enquiries

The Inland Revenue will correct any obvious mistakes fairly soon after your Return is filed. 'Enquiries' can be made at any time up to twelve months after the filing date (or date received if later). Cases will be chosen where it is considered that tax may be at risk. A certain number of cases will also be chosen at random. No reason will be given for an enquiry.

Penalties for late Returns

The penalties for late Returns are:

Returns not submitted by 31 January after tax year end – £100
Returns outstanding after a further six months   – Further £100

The above penalties are automatic but will be reduced if the tax owing is less. No penalties should normally arise for late Repayment Claims.

The Inland Revenue can apply to the Commissioners for further penalties to be levied of up to £60 per day. It may also issue a 'determination' of your tax bill in the absence of your Return; this will be referred to the Collector of Taxes for payment.

Tax payments

There are no more tax assessments under Self-Assessment. Instead you receive Statements of Account from the Inland Revenue.

Payments on account (based on the previous year's income tax liability) will usually be required in two equal instalments:

31 January in the tax year;
31 July following the end of the tax year.

A balancing payment (or repayment) will follow:

31 January after the end of the tax year (unless coded). This payment will coincide with the latest filing date for submission of your Tax Return.

Penalties and interest – late payment of tax

Interest will be payable if you claim to make reduced payments on account (which subsequently prove inadequate) or make an insufficient balancing payment.

- Surcharge (automatic):

Tax unpaid by 28 February (one month after the tax was due)	5% of unpaid tax
Tax unpaid by 31 July (six months after the tax was due)	Further 5% of unpaid tax

There are rights of appeal against these penalties if you think you have a reasonable excuse. However, it is not expected that the appeal procedure will have wide application.

In view of the automatic surcharges in the new regime you are strongly advised to make sure that your tax liabilities for each year are settled in full with the Inland Revenue by 31 January after each tax year end (and certainly by no later than 28 February).

Records

You are now required to keep proper records. This means three things:

- setting up adequate records in the first place

- maintaining them throughout the year

- retaining them for as long as necessary.

If adequate records are not kept the rules allow for a penalty of up to £3,000 to be charged.

Your records must be retained for a minimum period of time after the latest filing date for your Tax Return:

All taxpayers – twelve months after filing date
Self employed – five years after filing date

Where the Inland Revenue makes an enquiry into your Return you may exceptionally need to keep your records for a little longer.

A résumé of important dates

6 April 1996 onwards

All taxpayers need to keep proper records.

31 January 1998

The final deadline for filing the first Self-Assessment Tax Return for 1996/97 with the Inland Revenue and paying any balance of tax due for the year.

First payment on account of 1997/98 Income Tax.

6 April 1998

Self-Assessment Tax Returns for the 1997/98 tax year issued.

31 May 1998

Employers should provide a Form P60 (details of pay and tax paid) for 1997/98 to all employees.

6 July 1998

Employers should submit Forms P11D (return of benefits and expenses) for 1997/98 to the Inland Revenue and provide employees with a copy.

31 July 1998

Second payment on account of 1997/98 Income Tax. You should receive a further Statement of Account from the Inland Revenue to remind you.

30 September 1998

Deadline for taxpayers to file their Self-Assessment Tax Return (year ended 5 April 1998) if the Inland Revenue is to calculate the tax bill.

This is also the deadline for individuals taxed under PAYE to submit their Tax Returns if they have an underpayment of less than £1,000 which they would like collected through the following year's notice of coding (rather than pay in full on 31 January 1999).

31 January 1999

Final deadline for filing Self-Assessment Tax Return for 1997/98 with the Inland Revenue and paying any balance of tax due for the year. An automatic penalty of £100 will be charged for Tax Returns filed after this date.

Returns submitted after 30 September 1998 will normally have to include a calculation of the tax liability for the year.

First payment on account of 1998/99 Income Tax.

28 February 1999

A 5% automatic surcharge on any 1997/98 tax remaining unpaid. There will be a further 5% surcharge on any tax still remaining unpaid on 31 July 1999.

2

YOU AND THE INLAND REVENUE

Before we look at the different types of taxable income and the various allowances and reliefs you can claim, I thought it would be helpful to give you an outline of the functions of the Inland Revenue departments which operate our tax system. Overall authority for administering the legislation enacted by Government is vested in the Board of Inland Revenue. Although there are now many specialist departments within the Inland Revenue it is likely that your only direct contact with the Revenue will be through your Tax Office and the Collector of Taxes.

Tax Offices

There are many tax offices spread out all over the country. Each office is headed up by a District Inspector with a full support staff of Inspectors and Clerks. If you are either employed or a pensioner, your tax affairs will be looked after by the tax office which deals with the Pay-As-You-Earn affairs of your employer or his pension fund. Where you are self-employed you will find that your local tax office is responsible for your tax affairs.

Over recent years the Inland Revenue has been engaged in a fundamental reorganization of the local network of tax offices. In the new structure there are the following types of office:

• Taxpayer Service Office (TSO)

It is your TSO which sends you a Tax Return for you to complete each year. The same office processes your Return when you send it back. If any obvious or simple errors come to light you can expect to receive a notice from the TSO detailing the amendments that have been made to your Tax Return. If you are late sending in your Return you can initially expect to be chased up by your TSO. Providing you comply with all your tax obligations it is unlikely that you will have any involvement with the Inland Revenue other than through your TSO.

TSOs look after all the day-to-day tax matters of the many taxpayers whose income is taxed under Pay-As-You-Earn and whose tax affairs are unaffected by the system of Self-Assessment. In addition they are responsible for processing the business accounts of self-employed taxpayers.

6

- Tax District Office (TDO)

  In many parts of the country the TDO is in the same office block as the TSO. Apart from providing technical assistance to the local TSO the TDO is also responsible for the investigation of the Returns and business accounts of those taxpayers which are selected for further attention.

  If you are late in filing your Return or paying your taxes then, apart from in the London area, it will be your TDO which will start the enforcement and recovery action against you.

The Collector of Taxes

The only responsibility of the Collector of Taxes, as the name implies, is to collect the tax which is due from you.

You can provide for the payment of a future tax liability by purchasing a Certificate of Tax Deposit. Certificates can be bought from the Collector of Taxes. They earn interest from the date of purchase up until the normal due date for payment of the liability (see Chapter 15). The interest is taxable.

Communicating with the Inland Revenue

On any straightforward matter where it helps you to have a quick answer it is better to telephone your tax office. Unless you specifically ask to speak to the Inspector you will be put through to one of his assistants who will usually be able to answer your enquiry. On a more involved aspect of your tax affairs I suggest you write to the tax office. Always remember to quote your reference number in any correspondence. Unfortunately, you may sometimes have difficulty in understanding the reply to your letter. I hope that by the time you have read this book you will be in a better position to decipher any correspondence, which at first sight may seem horribly complicated.

There may be times when a particular matter concerning your tax affairs can best be resolved by a detailed discussion. This is the time to arrange a visit to your tax office. Where this is situated a long way from your place of employment or home you can always arrange to go to any local Inland Revenue office or your nearest Tax Enquiry Centre. The function of an Enquiry Centre is primarily to provide a call-in service for those taxpayers who prefer a face-to-face discussion with Inland Revenue staff. The address and telephone number of your nearest Tax Enquiry Centre are in your local phone book under Inland Revenue.

Alternatively you can call the Self-Assessment Helpline on 0645 000 444 for general advice and help. Calls are charged at local rate, and the Helpline is also open in the evenings and at weekends.

Determinations

As may be expected, the Inland Revenue has special powers to deal with taxpayers who have been sent a Return but fail to submit it by the filing date. In such circumstances the Inland Revenue can make a determination to the best of their knowledge and belief of an offending taxpayer's income and capital gains chargeable to tax. The actual amount of tax owing is worked out after taking into account estimates of:

- the taxpayer's allowances and reliefs;

- tax deducted at source on earnings and savings income.

Any determination can be superseded at a later date by a self-assessment whether this be by the taxpayer or by the Inland Revenue based on information provided by the taxpayer. Until then the determination counts as a self-assessment.

Enquiries

When your Return is received by your tax office it will be processed and then subjected to a comprehensive programme of checks. If there are any obvious errors in your return, for example in your arithmetic, these will be corrected by your tax office and no further enquiries will probably be made of you. But enquiries will be started if:

- your tax office thinks something requires fuller explanation;

- the Inland Revenue think there is a risk your Return may be incorrect;

- your Return is picked for enquiry at random.

Normally the Inland Revenue have 12 months from the filing date for your Return in which to tell you that it will be the subject of enquiries. A longer period of time is allowed if you send in your Return late. At the end of that period, if there have been no enquiries, your Return will normally become final. The Inland Revenue can then only reopen the matter if they discover an error which they could not reasonably have been expected to be aware of from the information provided in, or with, your Return.

Enquiries by local tax offices into Self-Assessment Tax Returns issued from April 1997 onwards should be conducted in accordance with the specific Code of Practice laid down by the Inland Revenue. This might be an occasion when you should exercise your right to be represented by a professional advisor.

Assessments and appeals

At the end of an enquiry into your Return the Inland Revenue will tell you what has been discovered and its effect upon your self-assessment Return.

You will also be advised of the additional tax payable by you or of any refund which might be due to you. You then have 30 days in which to amend your self-assessment. If you do not accept the Inland Revenue's offer to alter your own self-assessment your Inspector of Taxes does have the powers to make the amendment.

There are also two other circumstances, related to fraud or neglect, when your Inspector of Taxes can raise an assessment to collect tax which should have been paid on a self-assessment.

You do, of course, have a right of appeal to the Commissioners against an amendment to your Return or an assessment raised by your Tax Inspector. The procedure for resolving your appeal starts with a hearing before the General Tax Commissioners. It can then move on to the Courts and ultimately to the House of Lords.

The Taxpayer's Charter

The Taxpayer's Charter sets out the principles which the Inland Revenue aim to meet in handling taxpayers' affairs. It emphasizes the Inland Revenue's commitment to providing high quality customer service and highlights the help taxpayers can expect to receive, and the ways in which they can complain if they are not satisfied. Under the Charter, taxpayers can expect the Inland Revenue to be fair, helpful, efficient and accountable. The text of the Charter is as follows:

You are entitled to expect the Inland Revenue
To be fair

By settling your tax affairs impartially
By expecting you to pay only what is due under the law
By treating everyone with equal fairness

To help you

To get your tax affairs right
To understand your rights and obligations
By providing clear leaflets and forms
By giving you information and assistance at our enquiry offices
By being courteous at all times

To provide an efficient service

By settling your tax affairs promptly and accurately
By keeping your private affairs strictly confidential
By using the information you give us only as allowed by the law
By keeping to a minimum your costs of complying with the law
By keeping our costs down

To be accountable for what we do
By setting standards for ourselves and publishing how
well we live up to them

If you are not satisfied
We will tell you exactly how to complain
You can ask for your tax affairs to be looked at again
You can appeal to an independent tribunal
Your MP can refer your complaint to the Ombudsman

In return, we need you
To be honest
To give us accurate information
To pay your tax on time

Complaints

Most complaints about the Inland Revenue's handling of people's tax
affairs are satisfactorily settled by the local tax office concerned. Where
taxpayers are not satisfied with the response from the local office, they can
complain to:

- senior local management;

- the Inland Revenue's head office;

- a Member of Parliament;

- the Parliamentary Commission for Administration.

Taxpayers who are not satisfied with the Inland Revenue's response to
their complaints also have the option of putting their case to the Inland
Revenue Adjudicator. Complaints normally go to the Adjudicator only
when they have been considered by senior local management and if the
taxpayer is still not satisfied with the response he or she has received.
The Adjudicator will review all the facts and aim to reach a decision as
speedily as possible. Unless there are very exceptional circumstances the
Inland Revenue will normally accept the Adjudicator's decision.

The Adjudicator will consider complaints about the way in which
the Inland Revenue has handled someone's tax affairs – for example,
complaints about excessive delay, errors, discourtesy – or the way in
which the Inland Revenue has exercised discretion. The Board of Inland
Revenue receives an annual report from the Adjudicator which serves as
a useful mechanism for identifying areas where problems are occurring
and where changes may need to be considered.

Changes in legislation

Every year, the Chancellor of the Exchequer makes his annual Budget Statement. Not only does the Chancellor choose the occasion to introduce new or amending legislation to our tax laws, but he also announces the rates of tax and allowances for the following year.

The changes in legislation necessary to implement the Chancellor's proposals are subsequently published in a Finance Bill. The clauses in the Bill are debated and amendments are often proposed to some of them. Subsequently, the Bill is passed by both Houses of Parliament and receives the Royal Assent. It is then republished as a Finance Act.

It is the fiscal legislation passed by Parliament which is administered by the Inland Revenue. On occasions when the law is either unclear or ambiguous the Inland Revenue publish a Statement of Practice showing how they intend to interpret it. There are times when the Inland Revenue do not seek to apply the strict letter of the law. These are published as a list of Extra-Statutory Concessions.

The Inland Revenue also publish a number of booklets on different aspects of our tax system. A list of the most helpful booklets is set out in Table 1 at the end of the book.

Income Tax rates for 1997/98

Under our tax system, the tax (or fiscal) year runs from each 6 April to the following 5 April.

The rates of tax applying to taxable income for 1997/98 are:

Band of Taxable Income	Rate of Tax	Tax on Band	Cumulative Tax
£	%	£	£
0 – 4,100	20	820	820
4,101 – 26,100	23	5,060	5,880
over – 26,100	40		

The rate of 20% is known as the lower rate. The basic rate is 23% and tax at 40% is referred to as the higher rate.

The law provides that the bands of income taxable at the basic and higher rates are to be increased each tax year in line with the movement in the Retail Prices Index during the year to the end of September prior to the tax year. The Treasury can, however, order an increase different to the statutory commitment, providing Parliament agrees.

3

PERSONAL ALLOWANCES AND RELIEFS

Every taxpayer with an income from earnings or investments is entitled to claim the personal allowance, ensuring at least some income each year is free of tax.

The rates of the various personal allowances for 1997/98 are:

		£
Personal		4,045
Married couple's		*1,830
Additional personal		*1,830
Widow's bereavement		*1,830
Age		
• personal	(age 65-74)	5,220
• married couple's	(age 65-74)	*3,185
• personal	(age 75 and over)	5,400
• married couple's	(age 75 and over)	*3,225
Relief for blind person		1,280

*indicates allowances where tax relief is restricted to 15%.

There is a page in your Tax Return for you to claim the particular allowances to which you are entitled. The allowances on which tax relief is unrestricted are deducted from your total income in calculating the amount on which you pay Income Tax each year. Tax relief for the other allowances, highlighted by an asterisk in the above table, is given as a tax reduction.

Illustration
During 1997/98, Simon East, a married man, earned £14,200. His tax liability for the year is £1,938.15 as follows:

	£
Salary	14,200
Less: Personal allowance	4,045
Taxable income	£10,155
Income Tax Payable:	
£4,100 @ 20%	820.00
£6,055 @ 23%	1,392.65
	2,212.65
Less: £1,830 @ 15% (married couple's allowance)	274.50
	£1,938.15

The rates of allowances tend to vary from year to year. This is because the law provides that the allowances in the table above, are to go up at the beginning of each tax year. This upwards movement is in line with the increase in the Retail Prices Index during the year to the end of September prior to the tax year. The Treasury can, however, order an increase different from the statutory commitment providing Parliament agrees.

Personal allowance

Every man and woman, single or married, is entitled to the personal allowance. This can be of particular benefit to a married woman. She is able to set her personal allowance against a salary or business profits, investment income, or occupational and/or State Pension(s) including one paid to her based on her husband's contributions.

Married couple's allowance

A married man whose wife is living with him can claim the married couple's allowance. In the year of marriage the amount of the married couple's allowance depends upon the time during the year that the marriage took place. The allowance is reduced by one-twelfth for every complete month from 6 April up to the date of the wedding.

Illustration

Percy Hughes was married on 17 July 1997. He receives an allowance of £1,343 for 1997/98 calculated as follows:

	£
Married couple's allowance	1,830
Less: Reduction	
$3/_{12}$ x £1,830	457
1997/98 Allowance	£1,373

The married couple's allowance is not reduced in the year when couples separate or in the year of death of either spouse.

A wife can elect to receive one-half of the married couple's allowance. She does not need her husband's consent to make this election. Alternatively, the allowance can be deducted wholly from the wife's total income, instead of the husband's income. This sort of election must be made jointly by husband and wife. However, the husband can subsequently, on his own, elect to take back one-half of the allowance.

All the above elections refer only to the standard married couple's allowance of £1,830 and not to the age-related allowances. An election must be made on the special Inland Revenue Form 18. Any of the three elections must normally be made before the beginning of the tax year for which it is to have effect. It will then apply for that year and each succeeding tax year until altered by subsequent election or notice of withdrawal. A withdrawal is not effective until the tax year after that in which it is given to the Inland Revenue.

There are two exceptions to the time limit for making the elections. The first of these applies to the year of marriage where a notice can immediately be given in respect of the reduced married couple's allowance for that year. The second exception applies for the first tax year for which an election is made. Here an election may be made within the first 30 days of that tax year so long as the Inspector of Taxes was advised in writing before the start of the tax year of an intention to make the election.

If none of these elections is made, the husband is entitled to the full married couple's allowance. Where he has a sufficiently low taxable income and cannot make full use of his married couple's allowance he can transfer any excess allowance to his wife. Alternatively, if, following an election, a wife does not have sufficient taxable income against which to set off her married couple's allowance she can transfer the excess to her husband.

Age allowances

A pensioner whose income is below a specified annual limit is entitled to higher allowances: these are known as the personal age and married couple's age allowances. To be eligible the elderly taxpayer must be over the age of 65 during part or all of the tax year. There are higher age allowances for a pensioner over 75 for part or all of the tax year. The amount of the personal age allowance depends entirely on the age of the elderly taxpayer. So long as one spouse is at least 65 years old the husband will be due the married couple's age allowance. The level of this allowance depends on the age of the elder spouse.

Illustration

Albert White was 65 years old in 1997/98. His wife, Joan, enjoyed her 62nd birthday the same year. They are entitled to allowances of £8,405 and £4,045 as follows:

	Albert	Joan
	£	£
Personal age	5,220	4,045
Married couple's age	3,185	–
Total allowances	£8,405	£4,045

Another elderly couple, Frank and Jean Barrett, had their 73rd birthday (Frank) and 77th birthday (Jean) in 1997/98. Their total allowances are £8,445 and £5,400 as follows:

	Frank	Jean
	£	£
Personal age	5,220	5,400
Married couple's age	3,225	–
Total allowances	£8,445	£5,400

As the age allowances are designed to help those pensioners who are less well off, they reduce where their income before tax rises above £15,600 for 1997/98. This reduction in age allowances is one-half of the amount by which total income exceeds the stated limit of £15,600, although it cannot take the rate of the allowance below the level of either the single or married couple's allowances as the case may be. The personal age allowance is reduced before the married couple's age allowance.

Whether an elderly spouse can claim the personal age allowance depends solely on the amount of his or her income. However, any restriction of the married couple's age allowance is measured solely by the husband's income. It is never affected by the amount of the wife's income. Part of the husband's married couple's age allowance that is unused because, for example, he has a low income, can be transferred over to his wife in the same way that any unused part of the ordinary married couple's allowance can be transferred. However, the amount that can be made over to the wife is limited to the basic married couple's allowance – currently £1,830 for 1997/98. The excess must be set against the husband's income.

Illustration
Another elderly couple, James Flowers aged 79 and his wife Betty, aged 69, whose income amounted to £9,500 and £16,200 respectively during 1997/98 are entitled to allowances of £8,625 and £4,920 as follows:

	James	Betty
	£	£
Income before tax		
State pensions	3,247	1,942
Pensions from former employers	3,153	7,458
Investment income	3,100	6,800
	£9,500	£16,200

15

Allowances		
Personal age	5,400	5,220
Married couple's age	3,225	–
	£8,625	£5,220
Less: Reduction		
$1/2$ x £600 (£16,200 – £15,600)	–	300
1997/98 Allowances	£8,625	£4,920

It follows that no measure of personal age allowance is due to an elderly taxpayer (aged 65-74) whose income exceeds £17,950 for 1997/98. For a pensioner aged 75 or over the maximum income limit is increased to £18,310.

The upper income limits for a husband beyond which no measure of married couple's age allowance is due for 1997/98 are:

	Age of Elderly Spouse	
Husband's Age	*65-74*	*Over 74*
	£	£
Under 65	18,310	18,390
65-74	20,660	20,740
Over 74	–	21,100

The income limit for age allowances goes up each tax year in the same way as the main personal allowances.

Arising out of the transition to Independent Taxation a special personal allowance may be claimed in certain circumstances by a husband under 65 whose wife was aged 65-74 on 5 April 1990. This special personal allowance amounts to £3,400 for 1997/98. It increases to £3,540 if his wife was over 74 on 5 April 1994.

Additional personal allowance

To qualify for this allowance you must have at least one child living with you, who fulfills certain conditions and you must be

- single, or

- a widow or widower, or

- separated or divorced, or

- a married man whose wife cannot look after herself because she is either physically incapacitated or mentally infirm.

The child must be your own child, a step-child, or a child you have legally adopted before he or she reaches the age of 18. If the child is 16 or more years old at the start of the tax year he or she must be

- still at school, or

- attending a full-time course at a university, college or similar place of education, or

- undergoing a training course for at least two years with an employer in some trade or profession. A child who is on a two-year youth training programme will normally qualify.

Where the child living with you is not your own then he or she must be under 18 years old at the beginning of the tax year and looked after at your own expense.

No matter how many children you may have living with you who fulfil these tests only one allowance can be claimed. If more than one person is in a position to claim the allowance for the same child then it will be apportioned between them.

A man and a woman who are not married to each other but live together as man and wife are only entitled to the additional personal allowance for the youngest child living with them.

Only for the tax year in which a man, who is entitled to the additional personal allowance, marries can he choose whether to claim that allowance instead of the married couple's allowance. He will probably do so because this, unlike the married couple's allowance, is not reduced in the year of marriage. A husband with a low income will probably want to be given the reduced married couple's allowance because he can elect to transfer any unused part of this allowance to his wife, which he cannot do with the additional personal allowance.

In the year of separation there has always been the possibility, however remote, that someone could claim both the married couple's and additional personal allowances. Now that the married couple's allowance is more freely transferable between husband and wife, special rules, for the year of separation only, apply to limit the total allowance available. This is achieved by restricting the normal additional personal allowance where the claimant also receives the married couple's allowance.

Widow's bereavement allowance

Providing her husband was entitled to the married couple's allowance at the time of his death, a widow can claim this allowance for both the tax year in which her husband dies and the following tax year as long as she has not remarried by the beginning of that year.

In the year of her husband's death a widow can set all the allowances due to her against her total income for that tax year. For that year she cannot obtain both the bereavement allowance and a transferred married couple's allowance. However, if her husband's income was such that he could not use the full married couple's or married couple's age allowance then the balance will automatically be given to his widow.

Blind person's relief

This relief is given to a registered blind person. If both husband and wife are blind they may each claim the relief. If a husband or wife is unable to use up his or her blind person's relief fully because of insufficient income, any unused part of the relief can be transferred to the other spouse even if he or she is not blind.

When an individual first becomes entitled to the allowance, by being registered blind, the allowance will also be given for the previous year if, at the time, the individual had obtained the necessary proof of blindness required to qualify for registration. This prevents individuals losing out as a result of delays in the registration process.

Transfer of allowances

There are special rules to cater for a married couple who found that their total allowances were reduced when Independent Taxation was introduced. They apply to a couple who were married and living together in both 1989/90 and 1990/91 provided they did not elect for the wife's earnings to be separately taxed in 1989/90. Where the husband had a low income in 1990/91 and was unable to benefit from his full personal allowance he could elect to transfer his surplus personal allowance to his wife. He can also do so again in later years whenever he has an income which is insufficient to utilize his full personal allowance. However, where a husband's income for 1990/91 was such that he could benefit from his full personal allowance in that year he will never be able to transfer any part of his personal allowance to his wife.

Illustration

A young married couple, John and Samantha Carter, are substantially dependent on Samantha's salary. During 1997/98 she earned £14,000. John's salary was only £1,200. The married couple's and personal allowances which can be transferred to Samantha total £1,915 as follows:

Married couple's allowance

	£	£
Married couple's allowance		1,830
John's salary	1,200	
Less: Personal allowance	4,045	
		—
		£1,830

Personal allowances

	£	£
John's total allowances for 1989/90		7,160
Less: John's total income for 1997/98	1,200	
Samantha's total allowances for 1997/98 (including the transferred married couple's allowance)	5,875	
		7,075
		£85

These rules should not be confused with those which deal with the married couple's, married couple's age or blind person's allowances. These can be transferred in any tax year.

Relief on life assurance premiums

These days life assurance serves many purposes. They range from providing for the payment of lump sums on death, either to pay off the amount of an outstanding mortgage or to leave a lump sum for the deceased's dependants, to other uses which can often serve as tax-efficient forms of investment.

The amount of tax relief on premiums paid on qualifying life assurance policies is at the fixed rate of 12.5% on policies taken out before 14 March 1984. It should not be necessary for you to claim this since the premiums paid to the life assurance company are after deduction of the 12.5% tax relief. There are occasions when some or all of this relief can be withdrawn, and then a payment to the Inland Revenue will have to be made for the tax relief which has been lost. For example, the amount of such premiums which can be paid in any tax year without restriction of the tax relief is limited to £1,500 or one sixth of your total income before allowances, whichever is greater.

Illustration

Donald Kingsford pays annual qualifying life assurance premiums of £1,700 before tax relief. If his income is:

(a) £12,000, the 12.5% tax relief is unrestricted;

(b) £8,000, he will only receive the 12.5% tax relief on premiums of £1,500.

Premiums payable on a qualifying life assurance policy taken out after 13 March 1984 do not attract any tax relief. The same applies to future premiums payable on a similar policy taken out before that date if, after 13 March 1984, the benefits secured under the policy are varied or its terms extended.

4

INTEREST PAYMENTS AND OTHER OUTGOINGS

As the opportunities to claim tax relief for interest paid on borrowed money are limited, you should be aware of the few occasions when you can do so. These are:

- the purchase of property which is, at the time the interest is paid (or within 12 months from the date the loan was obtained), the only or main residence of the payer;

- the purchase, in certain circumstances, of life annuities if you are aged 65 or over;

- buying a share in

  - a partnership, or contributing capital to a partnership, if you are a partner;

  - a close company or lending capital to it;

  - an employee controlled company;

- buying plant and machinery for use in a job or partnership providing the plant and machinery attracts capital allowances for tax purposes.

It is important to appreciate that the purpose for which a loan is raised governs whether the interest on it will be eligible for tax relief. How the loan is secured is irrelevant.

Generally the interest on which tax relief is due is deducted from your total income in the year of payment. This general rule does not apply where you borrow money to buy either your home or a property which you let out: these are dealt with later on in the chapter.

Your own home

If you have borrowed money from a building society, a bank or some other source to help you buy your home you will receive tax relief on the interest you pay each year. Your home can be a house or a flat; it may even be a houseboat or a caravan.

It is not only the purchase price of your home which governs the maximum amount of the loan on which interest qualifies for tax relief. The incidental costs of buying your home such as surveyor's and solicitor's fees and stamp duty all count as part of the cost price of your home.

Interest relief is no longer given on new or replacement home improvement loans. However, interest on a home improvement loan, for example the installation of double glazing, taken out before 6 April 1988 still qualifies for tax relief.

There is an overall loan limit for mortgage interest tax relief: for 1997/98 this is £30,000. It applies to any one home rather than to each borrower. Unmarried couples jointly buying a home have to share the maximum limit between them.

Where two or more unmarried individuals share a home and each takes out a loan or has a share in a joint loan to purchase their home, the £30,000 limit is allocated between or amongst them in equal shares. For example, three individuals living together are each entitled to a limit of £10,000. Each individual qualifies for tax relief on the interest he or she pays on his or her loan or share of a joint loan up to £10,000. There are special rules to deal with unequal loans where the borrowers between them are not able to use up the full £30,000 limit, even though their total mortgages come to more than the limit.

Illustration

Courtney Griffiths, Sue Pearson and Joanna Moore share a terraced home they bought three years ago for £46,000. Courtney borrowed £18,000, Sue took out a loan for £8,000 whereas Joanna restricted her borrowing to only £6,000. Without a transfer of allowances the result would be:

Courtney gets tax relief on £10,000 with £8,000 unrelieved

Sue gets tax relief on	£8,000
Joanna gets tax relief on	£6,000
Total relief on	£24,000

Sue and Joanna can transfer relief on £2,000 and £4,000 respectively to Courtney, increasing his entitlement to relief on interest on a loan of £16,000. At the end of the day interest on £30,000 of the total borrowing by all three friends of £32,000 qualifies for tax relief.

Mortgages taken out before the beginning of August 1988 are unaffected by these rules. In these cases the limit of £30,000 applies to each borrower.

Married couples can share their mortgage interest tax relief in any way they want by completing an allocation of interest election. An election for the 1997/98 tax year can be made at any time up to 31 January 2000 or within such longer period as the Board of Inland Revenue may in any particular case allow. It will then also apply for 1998/99 unless the couple jointly elect on or before 31 January 2000 to withdraw it. In its first year of operation an election cannot be retracted once it has been made.

You can continue to claim tax relief on your mortgage interest if you are away from home for any of the following reasons:

- you are employed in some capacity that requires you to live in accommodation provided by your employer, in certain specific circumstances. The same applies if you are self-employed and the terms of your trade or profession are such that you must live in accommodation provided for your use;

- you are temporarily absent from your home for up to 1 year;

- you are required by your employer to move to another place of work in the UK or abroad. In order that the tax relief on a loan to buy your home can be maintained it must be anticipated that you will go back there on your return. Furthermore your absence should not be expected to last for more than 4 years;

- you have put your present home up for sale but have found it impossible to arrange that the sale coincides with the purchase of your new home. To overcome such difficulties, borrowers moving home, who are unable to sell their existing homes, can continue to claim mortgage interest relief in respect of their old home. They are allowed this relief for a period of up to 1 year (or longer at the Inland Revenue's discretion) after moving out. Nor do they have to take out a mortgage on their new home.

Some borrowers are still faced with mortgages which exceed the value of their homes. If they want to move they cannot pay off all the outstanding mortgage out of the sale proceeds of their home. It is now easier for borrowers with negative equity in their homes to move on. Lenders can keep the old loan in existence, rather than having to redeem it and advancing a new one, without the borrower losing entitlement to mortgage interest relief. The amount of the deemed new mortgage on which interest ranks for tax relief, subject to the overall limitation of £30,000, is the lower of the outstanding mortgage and the purchase price of the new home.

Where part of a borrower's home is let or used for business, a mortgage can be treated as though it is two separate loans. Normal mortgage interest relief can be claimed for the part attributable to the residential use of the property. The interest on the loan relating to the let proportion or business usage of the home can either be set against the rental income received or allowed as a deduction in the profits of the business, as the case may be.

Most of you are making your regular mortgage repayments after deduction of tax on the interest element in each repayment. This procedure is known as 'Mortgage Interest Relief at Source' – MIRAS for short. The rate of tax relief on mortgage interest is 15% for 1997/98. You do not have to pay this tax over to the Inland Revenue. This applies even where you have no taxable income, or where your income is less than your personal allowances. If your mortgage exceeds the limitation of £30,000 on which interest qualifies for tax relief you will receive relief on that part of the total interest payable equivalent to this limit. This relief is obtained either through the tax deduction scheme or your PAYE coding.

If part of your home is let, you can take the tax relief on the interest on any mortgage to buy the home in one of two ways, either under MIRAS or as a deduction against the rental income you receive. You can choose whichever basis you prefer. Furthermore, if you are presently within the MIRAS scheme, and want to opt out so that you can receive tax relief under the rules for rented properties, you must notify your Inspector of Taxes of your wish to come out of the MIRAS scheme within 22 months of the end of the tax year in which you want the new arrangement to begin. Once made, this election is irrevocable.

Home annuity loans

The main residence mortgage rules, including the £30,000 limitation, also apply to loans used to purchase an annuity from an insurance company. The borrower must be at least 65 years old. Not less than 90% of the loan on which the interest is payable must go towards buying an annuity for life. Security for the loan must be the borrower's main residence. Interest on home annuity loans continues to attract tax relief at the basic rate of 23%.

A home for a dependent relative

It is no longer possible to get tax relief on a mortgage, within the overall £30,000 limit, taken out to buy a home for a dependent relative. This change applied to new and replacement loans taken out on or after 6 April 1988. Tax relief is preserved on existing qualifying loans.

The relative must be either a pensioner or too unwell to look after himself or herself. Where the relative is the claimant's mother or mother-in-law, it is sufficient if she is widowed, separated or divorced.

Let property

Interest on a loan taken out to buy or improve a property which you rent out is tax deductible. The interest is set against the rental income from the property. Should the interest payable in a tax year exceed the rents receivable in the same year, the loss can only be carried forward to future years.

Illustration

Paul Green bought a property in 1988 with the assistance of a £60,000 loan. He lets it out and the rents less expenses came to £7,000 and £12,000 during 1996/97 and 1997/98 respectively.

	1996/97		1997/98
	£	£	£
Rents less expenses	7,000		12,000
Less: Loan interest paid	9,000	6,600	
Loss carried forward	£2,000	2,000	
			8,600
1997/98 Taxable Income			£3,400

Business loans

Most businesses need to borrow money at some time for one purpose or another. Interest on any such borrowings is allowable as a deduction against your business profits providing the borrowed money is used for business purposes. It does not matter for this purpose whether the borrowings arise because your bank account goes overdrawn, or because you take out a loan for some specific purpose connected with your business.

If you need to borrow to buy an asset – such as a car or a piece of machinery – for use in your business, the interest you pay will qualify for tax relief but will be restricted where the asset is also used privately.

If you are about to become a member of a partnership, you may need to borrow money to purchase a share in the partnership or to contribute capital for use in its business. If that is the case, the interest on the borrowings will qualify for tax relief.

Alternatively, you may have business connections with a private company. The interest on a loan raised so you can either acquire shares in the company or lend it money for use in its business will qualify for tax relief. You must either own at least 5% of the company's share capital or have at least some shareholding and work for the greater part of your time in the business.

Employees who need to borrow to buy shares in their company as part of an employee buy-out are allowed tax relief on the interest.

Charitable deeds of covenant

Deeds of covenant are an effective way of making a donation to a charity. To be valid for tax purposes, a deed must be capable of providing for regular annual payments over a minimum period of more than three years. The payer must deduct Income Tax at the basic rate from every payment under a deed. The tax deducted can be retained providing the payer has suffered tax at the basic rate which is at least equivalent to the tax deducted from all covenanted payments during a tax year.

As an incentive to individuals with high incomes, they are allowed to deduct covenanted payments to charities from their income in calculating their tax liabilities at the higher rate of 40%.

Tax relief on charitable deeds of covenant is only allowed against the payer's income. If the payer is not liable to Income Tax on his or her income alone, payments under a charitable deed of covenant may not qualify for tax relief. One way of overcoming this situation is to switch the covenant to the tax-paying spouse.

Quite often individuals making covenants do not draw them up in a form which is legally effective. To help charities and individual donors ensure that their covenants are legally effective, guidance notes are available from the Inland Revenue. They suggest model forms of words which charities and individuals may use if they so wish and deal with a number of other practical points about the conditions which covenants must satisfy to be eligible for tax relief.

Gift Aid

Gift Aid is an Income Tax relief for single cash gifts by individuals to charities. Each gift must be at least £250, net of basic rate tax. There is no maximum annual limit for gifts by any one donor. As with regular donations to charities under deed of covenant, payments under the Gift Aid Scheme are made net of tax at the basic rate. You must give the charity a certificate – Form R190 (SD) – for each separate payment so it can claim the tax back from the Inland Revenue. Individuals with high incomes can deduct their gifts from their income in calculating how much tax they must pay at the top 40% tax rate.

Gifts in kind are not allowed – only cash gifts. Gifts will not qualify for the relief if they are linked with any purchase of property by the charity from the donor or where they are in return for services or benefits.

Payroll deduction scheme

If you are in employment there may be a further alternative way open for you to make donations to charity. This depends on your employer operating such a scheme through an Approved Agency Charity. Then your charitable donations can be made through your employer by way of regular deductions from your salary. Employers are not bound to launch such schemes and employees can choose whether to participate in them. If you do so, you will be entitled to tax relief on donations not exceeding £1,200 annually.

Private medical insurance

Tax relief has been withdrawn on premiums for private medical insurance for individuals aged 60 and over. This applies to contracts taken out on or after 2 July 1997. Premiums on annual contracts taken out before this date continue to qualify for relief until they come to an end.

For joint contracts covering a husband and wife then only one of them needed to be over 60. Relief was available to the individual who actually paid the premium whether it was for himself, a relative or friend. The rate of tax relief was limited to the basic rate of 23%. This relief was given wholly by deduction from the amount of the premium due.

Vocational training

You can get tax relief on payments you make for your own vocational training. The training costs which qualify for this tax relief must lead to a National Vocational Qualification, or the Scottish equivalent, up to and including level 5. However, the relief does not extend to general education qualifications, such as GCSEs or 'A' levels, even where these are taken as a preliminary to Vocational Qualification Study. Nor is tax relief allowed to children under 16, and 16–18 year-olds in full-time schooling. The same applies for training undertaken wholly or mainly for recreational purposes or as a leisure activity.

There are two other conditions which have to be satisfied by the trainee. Firstly, you must be a UK resident. Secondly, you must not be getting, or eligible for, assistance under Government Schemes such as student grant awards or employment training. However, trainees with Career Development loans or 'access funding' qualify for the relief.

The relief is given on study, examination or assessment costs. Not covered are the cost of books or equipment nor travelling and subsistence expenses.

If you are over the age of 30 and pay for your own retraining for a new career, you will be allowed relief from Income Tax on fees paid to training providers for full-time vocational courses, lasting between four weeks and a year. It is not necessary for the courses to lead to qualifications.

You get the relief directly when paying your fees. All you have to do is deduct an amount equal to the basic rate of tax of 23% from the study, examination or assessment fees you pay. You can get this relief even if you are a non-taxpayer. Also, higher rate taxpayers will be allowed relief on their vocational training costs at the top rate of 40%.

5

EARNINGS FROM EMPLOYMENT

Most of you will be familiar with at least some part or other of the Pay-As-You-Earn (PAYE) system. It provides a mechanism for collecting the tax due on the earnings of those people in employment. Employers must deduct Income Tax from the earnings of their employees and every month the total of these deductions has to be paid over to the Inland Revenue. The PAYE taken off an employee's earnings is treated as a credit against the overall amount of tax payable by the employee for the tax year in question. In working out the amount of tax to deduct from each employee's salary or pay packet, the employer takes into account each individual's own allowances and other reliefs. This is possible because the Inland Revenue issue employers with a code number for each employee. In turn the code number incorporates each employee's allowances and reliefs. The system allows for these to be spread evenly throughout the tax year to avoid any substantial variation in the amount of tax deducted from each salary cheque or pay packet.

The sort of earnings which count as taxable income from an employment are:

An annual salary or wage
Bonus
Overtime
Commission
Tips or gratuities
Holiday pay
Sick pay
Earnings from a part-time employment
Directors' fees or other remuneration
Benefits-in-kind

All directors and employees are taxed on the earnings they actually receive in a tax year.

Code numbers

I have already mentioned that each employee is issued with a code number by the tax office. In theory the code number should ensure that the correct amount of tax has been deducted from your earnings by the end of the tax year. The system can only work properly and effectively if your local tax office is kept informed of any changes in your personal circumstances which affect the amount of your allowances or reliefs.

For example, most if not all notices of coding for the 1998/99 tax year commencing on 6 April 1998 were issued during the early part of the year. This was before taxpayers came to complete their 1998 Tax Returns. The Return requires a report of each person's income, capital gains, reliefs and allowances for the tax year just finished – the year to 5 April 1998. It follows that the information on which all the code numbers for 1998/99 have been based is out of date. This is why it is important you should check your code number for 1998/99 and write to your tax office setting out any alterations that are required to your allowances or reliefs. If the rate of any allowance has been altered in the Budget there is no need for you to communicate with your tax office. Employees who only receive the personal allowance will have their code adjusted automatically by their employer or pension provider in accordance with instructions issued by their tax office. Only if a notice of coding is needed for some other reason will they be sent one. All other employees who get the married couple's and related allowances will be sent a new coding notice.

On the following page is an illustration of a notice of coding for David Jones for 1998/99. It shows he is a married man. His allowances for 1998/99 are £5,875 before deductions. The first three of these relate to benefits-in-kind in the form of a company car and private medical insurance cover provided by David's employer. Some of the types of taxable expenses and benefits are dealt with later on in the chapter. The coding notice illustrates how the tax payable on benefits-in-kind is usually collected. This is done by restricting David's allowances by the value of the benefits-in-kind. In the illustration they come to £4,090, reducing the allowances to £1,785.

Some of the allowances only attract tax relief at the fixed rate of 15%. This applies for all taxpayers. The allowances subject to this restriction are the married couple's, the two age-related married couple's, the additional personal and the widow's bereavement. Also affected is the relief for maintenance payments mentioned in Chapter 11. The fourth deduction in the coding notice illustrates the procedure for collecting the right amount of tax from David on his married couple's allowance. By restricting the net allowance to an effective amount of £1,194 (£1,830 – £636) he will receive tax relief of £274.50 (£1,194 @ 23%) assuming he is a basic rate taxpayer. This is equivalent to the fixed rate of 15% on the full allowance of £1,830. If he were a 40% taxpayer the allowance restriction would be increased to £1,144. The final deduction is for tax underpaid for 1996/97 of £115. For any one of a number of reasons the allowances given, or deductions made, in David's coding notice may subsequently turn out to be incorrect. If, as a result, there is an underpayment of tax, this is usually collected in a later year, again by restricting allowances in the coding. In our illustration a reduction in

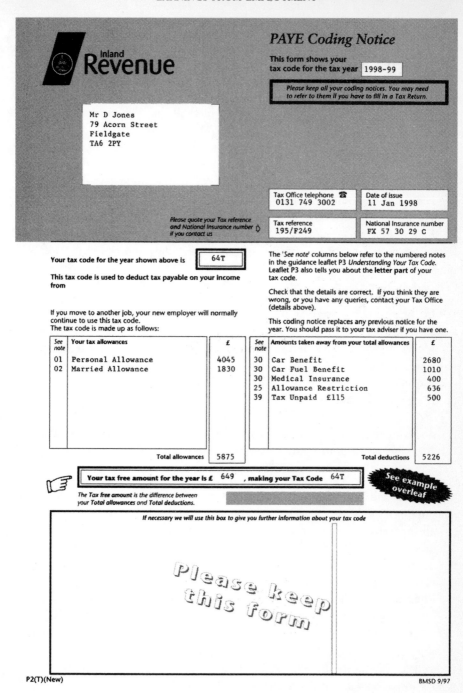

PAYE Coding Notice

This form shows your tax code for the tax year **1998-99**

Please keep all your coding notices. You may need to refer to them if you have to fill in a Tax Return.

Mr D Jones
79 Acorn Street
Fieldgate
TA6 2PY

Tax Office telephone ☎ 0131 749 3002	Date of issue 11 Jan 1998

Please quote your Tax reference and National Insurance number if you contact us

Tax reference 195/F249	National Insurance number FX 57 30 29 C

Your tax code for the year shown above is 64T

This tax code is used to deduct tax payable on your income from

If you move to another job, your new employer will normally continue to use this tax code.
The tax code is made up as follows:

The '*See note*' columns below refer to the numbered notes in the guidance leaflet P3 *Understanding Your Tax Code*. Leaflet P3 also tells you about the **letter part** of your tax code.

Check that the details are correct. If you think they are wrong, or you have any queries, contact your Tax Office (details above).

This coding notice replaces any previous notice for the year. You should pass it to your tax adviser if you have one.

See note	Your tax allowances	£	See note	Amounts taken away from your total allowances	£
01	Personal Allowance	4045	30	Car Benefit	2680
02	Married Allowance	1830	30	Car Fuel Benefit	1010
			30	Medical Insurance	400
			25	Allowance Restriction	636
			39	Tax Unpaid £115	500
	Total allowances	5875		**Total deductions**	5226

Your tax free amount for the year is £ 649 **, making your Tax Code** 64T

The Tax free amount is the difference between your Total allowances and Total deductions.

See example overleaf

If necessary we will use this box to give you further information about your tax code

Please keep this form

P2(T)(New)

BMSD 9/97

allowances for 1998/99 of £500 will result in the Inland Revenue collecting the underpayment of £115 (£500 @ 23%) from David during the year. A similar sort of adjustment to your coding notice for 1998/99 will also be made if you sent your Tax Return for the year to 5 April

1997 back to your Tax Office by 30 September 1997 and asked to pay your tax owing for the year (less than £1000) through the PAYE system.

The combined effect of these adjustments is to leave David with allowances of only £649 to be set against his salary for 1998/99. His code number will be 64T. Clearly, there is a direct link between David's allowances and his code number. The suffix letter is added to the coding as a means of identifying the category into which a taxpayer falls. The various letters which can be part of the coding and what they stand for are as follows:

- L – is for a code which includes the personal allowance;

- H – stands for a code with the personal allowance plus either the married couple's allowance or the additional personal allowance;

- P – is for a code with the personal allowance for those aged 65-74;

- V – indicates the pensioner is entitled to both the personal and married couple's allowances for ages 65-74;

- T – applies in most other cases, for example:
    - You ask your tax office not to use the letters L, H, P or V.
    - You are due a personal or married couple's allowance for age 75 and over.
    - You are not entitled to the full higher age-related allowance because your total income exceeds £15,600.
    - You have a deduction from your allowances in your code for an item such as a car benefit.

There are also a number of other codes:

- OT – no allowances have been given to you. Tax will be deducted at the lower rate, then the basic rate, and finally at the higher rate of 40%, depending on your income;

- BR – this is an instruction for your employer to deduct tax at the basic rate;

- NT – this means that no tax will be deducted;

- DO – tax will be deducted at the higher rate of 40%;

- Prefix K – a K code is given to employees whose taxable benefits exceed their personal allowances. The amount of the negative allowances is then added to the pay on which tax is to be paid. This system of K codes is designed to make taxpayers pay all the tax due on their benefits evenly throughout the tax year under the PAYE system, instead of receiving a demand at the end of the tax year for the lump sum owing.

Forms P60

Shortly after the end of each tax year every employer sends in to the Inland Revenue a Return summarizing the names of all employees, their earnings during the tax year, and the deductions made for both Income Tax and National Insurance Contributions. By 31 May following the end of a tax year your employer must hand you a Form P60. This is a certificate of your earnings for the past tax year incorporating the Income Tax and National Insurance Contributions you paid. For most employees the Income Tax withheld under PAYE corresponds with the tax due on their earnings. Below is an illustration of the Form P60 sent to David

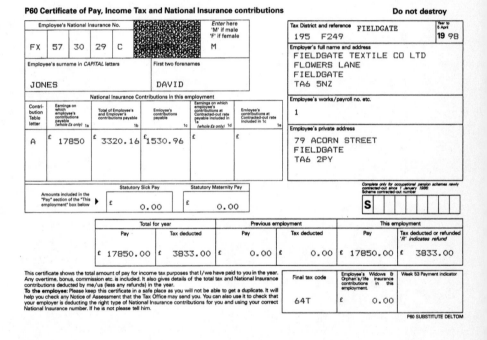

Jones by his employer for 1997/98. This shows that the tax deducted from his earnings in the year amounted to £3833.00 based on a tax code of 64T. It also tells him that he suffered National Insurance Contributions of £1,530.96 in 1997/98.

Changing your job

Whenever you change your job your employer will hand you Parts 1A, 2 and 3 of a Form P45. This form details your name and address, the name and address of your employer, your tax district and reference number, and your code number at the date of leaving. It also shows your cumulative salary and tax deductions for the tax year up to the date that you leave, and your salary and tax deductions from the last employment unless this information is the same as the cumulative figures. Your employer will send the first part of the P45 form to his tax district.

You must hand Parts 2 and 3 of the Form P45 to your new employer. He will enter your address and the date you start your new job before sending Part 3 of the form to his own tax office. The information on the form enables your new employer to make the right deductions for Income Tax and National Insurance from your new salary or wage.

You should keep Part 1A of the form for your own records. If necessary, it can then be used to assist you in the preparation of your own tax return.

Should you not have a P45 to hand to your new employer, you will find that the deductions from your salary for Income Tax are equivalent to those of a single person without any other allowances or reliefs. This is known as the 'emergency' basis. Where this happens you should either ask for and complete a Tax Return or send in sufficient information to your new employer's tax office so that the correct code number can be sent to your employer. If you have just left school or are taking up employment for the first time you should complete either a Form P15 or a Form P46 as a way of making sure that the right deductions for Income Tax are made from your wage or salary.

Expenses

The rules which allow you to claim tax relief on expenses relating to an employment are extremely restrictive. They seek to deny tax relief on almost all types of expenses which are not ultimately borne by the employer. This is because the employee has to show that any expenditure is incurred 'wholly, exclusively and necessarily' while performing the duties of the employment. If the employer has not been prepared to foot the bill for the expenditure involved, then the Inland Revenue are likely to take the view it was incurred more as a matter of choice than of necessity. Nevertheless, some business expenses paid personally are deductible from your income. Details of these should be entered on your Tax Return. They include:

- annual subscriptions to a professional body;

- business use of your own car and telephone;

- clothing and upkeep of tools – the Inland Revenue and the Trade Unions have agreed flat rate allowances for the upkeep of tools and special clothing for most classes of industry. The current rates are set out in Table 2. As an alternative you may claim a deduction for the actual expenses on these items;

- payment by directors or employees for work-related insurance cover. Tax relief is also allowed on meeting the cost of uninsured liabilities.

Remember that the cost of travelling between your home and the office is not allowable for tax purposes.

Most expenses you incur in your job or employment are probably borne by your employer, who either reimburses you on an expense claim or pays for them direct. Tax free for everyone are:

- luncheon vouchers up to 15p per day;

- free or subsidized meals in a staff canteen, providing the facilities can be used by all staff;

- sporting and recreational facilities;

- staff parties, providing the annual cost to the employer is no more than £75 per head;

- routine health checks or medical screening;

- awards for long service of at least 20 years. The cost of the articles purchased by the employer must not exceed £20 for each year of service;

- gifts not exceeding £150 in a tax year to an employee from a third party – by reason of his or her employment;

- out-placement counselling costs;

- child-care facilities provided by an employer at the work place or elsewhere (but not on domestic premises);

- car-parking facilities at or near your place of work;

- the cost of infrequent private transport when you have been working late and either public transport is no longer available or it would be unreasonable to expect you to use it at a late hour. Infrequent late working means a requirement to work until at least 9.00 p.m. not more than 60 times in a tax year;

- mileage allowances paid by an employer where employees use their car on business providing the mileage rate does no more than reimburse employees for the costs they have incurred on business travel. The tax-free rates laid down by the Inland Revenue for 1997/98 are:

| Engine Size – cc | Business Use | |
	First 4,000 miles	Excess
Up to 1000	28p	17p
1001 to 1500	35p	20p
1501 to 2000	45p	25p
Over 2000	63p	36p

If an employer chooses to pay a uniform rate this should be the average of the middle two rates i.e. 40p and 22.5p. Employees are taxed on payments made by their employers over and above the rates in the table.

- personal incidental expenses when you stay away from home overnight on business. The most common expenses covered are newspapers, telephone calls to home, and laundry. The tax-free limits, including VAT, are £5.00 per night for overnight stays anywhere within the United Kingdom and £10 per night for overnight stays elsewhere. Where an employer exceeds these limits, the whole of the payment becomes taxable – not just the excess.

Employees (including full-time working directors who own 5% or under of the company's shares) earning less than £8,500 per annum including expenses are not taxed on most benefits or perks provided by their employers. In addition to those in the above list, the most valuable non-taxable benefits for this type of employee are private medical insurance and a company car.

Other directors and employees (including full-time working directors), whose total earnings, including expenses, exceed £8,500 per annum, are generally taxed on the actual value of any benefits and taxable expenses obtained from their employments. Information about your expense payments and benefits-in-kind is supplied by your employer to your tax office annually on a Form P11D. Your employer is required to give you a copy of this form by 6 July following the end of the tax year. It represents your employer's calculations of your taxable payments and cash equivalents of benefits-in-kind. It is down to you to justify those on which you should not be taxed. This should not cause you any difficulties where the expenses, such as travelling and entertaining, have genuinely arisen from the performances of the duties of your employment.

There are set rules for calculating some benefits.

(a) Company cars
Generally regarded as the most valuable and sought-after benefit, it is based on the price of the company car.

The car benefit charge is 35% of the list price of the car. It is reduced by one-third where you do between 2,500 and 17,999 miles a year on business. If your business mileage comes to 18,000 or more the reduction increases to two-thirds. The car benefit is even less for cars which are four or more years old at the end of a tax year. There is then a further reduction of one-third after business mileage has been taken into account.

Illustration

A car was first registered in August 1992. The list price at the time was £9,500. Carol Latchford does 13,000 miles on business during the tax year. Her taxable benefit amounts to £1,478 calculated as follows:

	£
Car benefit: 35% of list price	3,325
Deduction for business mileage: one-third	1,108
	2,217
Less: Reduction for age of car: one-third	739
Taxable Benefit	£1,478

The 2,500 and 18,000 mileage limits are proportionately reduced if your company car is not available to you for the full tax year. No discounts are given on second cars unless you do at least 18,000 miles on business in that car. The reduction is then one-third.

Any contribution, up to a maximum amount of £5,000, you make towards the purchase price of the car or accessories reduces the list price on which the taxable benefit is calculated.

Illustration

The list price of Oliver Sim's new company car is £14,200. He contributes an amount of £3,200 towards the purchase. The price of his car for tax purposes is £11,000.

For the purpose of these new rules the list price of a car will usually be the total of:

- manufacturer's, importer's or distributor's list price of the car on the day before the date of registration;

- taxes, excluding the Road Fund Licence;

- delivery charges, including VAT;

- the list price of any accessory fitted before the car is made available to an employee, including VAT and any delivery or fitting charges;

- the list price of any accessory or set of accessories (for example alloy wheels) over £100 (including VAT, fitting and delivery) fitted after the car is made available to an employee. This only applies for accessories fitted after 31 July 1993. Where the price of an employee's car is increased for accessories fitted after the car was made available to him, the increased price applies from the beginning of the tax year in which they were fitted and subsequent years.

Both the cost of converting a company car for use by a disabled person and the addition of extra-cost options, such as automatic transmission and power steering, are not counted as accessories in working out the taxable benefit for a disabled employee.

There is an upper limit of £80,000 on the price of a car for the purpose of calculating the taxable benefit. Where the list price of a car exceeds this figure, the price for tax purposes will be £80,000.

Mileage between your home and place of business counts as private, not business usage.

Home-to-work travel in a car made available by an employer is not regarded as private use where:

- the employee has a travelling appointment;

- the employee travels from home to a temporary place of work and the distance travelled is less than the distance between the normal place of work and the temporary place of work;

- exceptionally, the home qualifies under tax law as a place of work and the employee travels from home to another place of work in the performance of his duties.

There are also circumstances where home-to-work travel in a car provided by an employer is regarded as private use but is ignored for tax purposes. These are where:

- a disabled person is provided with a car for home-to-work travel and there is no other private use;

- a car is provided for home-to-work travel when public transport is disrupted;

- a car is provided for late night journeys from work to home;

- the car is from an employer's car pool and any home-to-work travel is merely incidental to its business use. The car must not be garaged at or near the employee's home overnight.

If it is the company's policy to meet the cost of fuel for private motoring there is an additional taxable benefit. Again it is based on predetermined fixed amounts dependent on the cubic capacity of the company car. For 1997/98 the scale of benefits, incorporating the separate scale charge for diesel is:

Engine Size – cc	Petrol	Diesel
	£	£
1400 or less	800	740
1401 to 2000	1,010	740
Over 2000	1,490	940

(b) Mobile telephones

There is also a fixed benefit to cover the private use of a mobile telephone provided by an employer. For 1997/98 an employee will pay Income Tax on the standard amount of £200 for each mobile telephone. This amount can be reduced where the mobile telephone is not available for the full tax year. An employee can escape this tax charge altogether if no private calls are made on the mobile telephone or if the employer is reimbursed for the full cost of the private use. A call is not considered a private call where it is made for business reasons but contains an incidental, non-business element.

(c) Company vans

Also taxable on a fixed amount is an employee to whom a company van is made available for private use, again including travel between home and work. For 1997/98 the taxable benefit is £500 for a van under four years old at the end of the tax year. For an older van the amount on which you pay tax is reduced to £350. Both fixed benefits also cover the cost of any fuel provided for private motoring. As with company cars, the use of a van from an employer's van pool should not normally give rise to a tax charge. These rules apply to a company van with a design weight up to 3500 kilograms. There is no taxable benefit on the incidental private use of a heavy commercial vehicle with a design weight exceeding 3500 kilograms.

(d) Living accommodation

In some trades it is established practice for the employer to provide living accommodation. This can also be desirable where there is a security risk. No Income Tax liability arises in either sort of situation.

In other circumstances Income Tax is chargeable on the annual value of the property after deducting any rent paid for it. The annual value of property for these purposes is broadly equivalent to the gross rateable value. Estimated rateable values will be used for new properties which do not appear on the domestic rating lists. An additional tax charge must be faced where the accommodation costs more than £75,000. This is worked out by applying the Inland Revenue's official interest rate (see below) at the beginning of the tax year to the excess of the cost price over £75,000.

(e) Beneficial loans

Loans from an employer which are either interest free or where the interest charged by the employer is below a commercial rate can give rise to a taxable benefit. The benefit is calculated by applying the Inland Revenue's official rate of interest to the loan. At the time of going into print the rate is 7.25%. The benefit is reduced by any interest actually paid on the loan. No charge to tax arises where all an employee's cheap or interest-free loans, excluding loans which qualify for tax relief, total no more than £5,000. A tax charge is also avoided where the loan is for a purpose on which the interest would qualify for tax relief (see Chapter 4).

(f) Medical insurance

You will be taxed on private medical insurance premiums paid by your employer for you or other members of your family. If you go abroad on business then the cost of medical insurance cover, or actual medical treatment overseas, is not taxable on you as a benefit.

(g) Relocation expenses

An employee who changes his job, or is relocated by his employer, is not taxable on the costs of a relocation package up to £8,000. This limit applies to each job-related move. There are specific definitions for the removal expenses and benefits which qualify for exemption within the monetary limit.

Employee share ownership

The first type of all-employee approved share scheme is the savings-related share option scheme. This sort of scheme operates in combination with either a bank or building society SAYE savings contract under which employees save a fixed regular amount each month. The maximum amount that can be saved is £250 per month over either a three- or five-year period. The price at which options can be offered to directors and employees cannot be less than 80% of the market value of the shares at the time the options are granted. The receipt of the options and any increase in the value of the shares between the time that the options are granted and the date when they are exercised are free of Income Tax.

Under an approved profit-sharing scheme a company makes an allocation of profits to trustees who, in turn, use the contribution in acquiring shares in the company which are subsequently allotted to employees. The limit on the market value of shares which may be appropriated to any one individual in each tax year is 10% of salary with a minimum limit of £3,000 and a maximum of £8,000. There is no Income Tax liability when the shares are set aside nor if they are retained by the trustees of the scheme for three years.

No liability to Income Tax is imposed on a director or employee who aquires, or disposes of, ordinary shares under his employer's company share option plan. The market value of shares, at the time of the grant of the option, over which an individual holds unexercised rights under the plan must not exceed £30,000. An option must be exercised not less than three, or more than ten, years after it is granted, nor under three years after a previous exercise. The gain is measured by the difference between the sale proceeds and the cost of acquiring the shares, and is charged to Capital Gains Tax at the time of disposal. The price payable must be fixed at the time of the grant and must not be less than the market value of the shares at that date. Options granted before 17 July 1995 under then approved schemes continue to qualify for tax relief on exercise even if they exceed the £30,000 ceiling applying to company share option plans.

There are other forms of unapproved share option and share incentive schemes as well as employee share ownership trusts, but it is outside the scope of this book to go into these in detail.

Profit-related pay

Profit-related pay is that part of an employee's pay which is linked to the profits of his or her employer. All PRP is free of Income Tax up to the point where PRP is either 20% of pay or £4,000 a year, whichever is lower. This relief is worth as much as £920 per annum for a basic rate taxpayer and up to £1,600 annually for a higher rate taxpayer. Your tax relief is passed on to you through your employer's PAYE scheme. Relief only applies to PRP payments made under a scheme registered by an employer with the Inland Revenue.

The relief is being gradually phased out such that for profit periods beginning:

- before 1 January 1998, there will be no change in the £4,000 ceiling on relief;

- between 1 January and 31 December 1998, the ceiling will be reduced to £2,000;

- between 1 January and 31 December 1999, the ceiling will come down to £1,000;

- on or after 1 January 2000, no relief will be available.

Payments on termination of employment

It is common practice for an employee to be paid a lump sum on the termination of an employment. If the right to receive the payment arose during the period of employment then it is taxable in full in the same way as other earnings. Otherwise the lump sum payment is either wholly or partly tax free. The occasions when the payments are free of tax are:

- where the employment ceases because of the accidental death, injury or disability of the employee;

- where most of the employee's time was spent working overseas for the employer;

- where the lump sum payment is made at a time other than on death or retirement. The first £30,000 is then tax free. Only the excess of any payment over £30,000 is taxable.

Any statutory redundancy payment you receive, although exempt from tax itself, has to be counted in with any other lump sum payment from your employer in working out the tax due on the lump sum.

6

VALUE ADDED TAX

Value Added Tax (VAT) is a tax on supplies of goods and services. It is not the 'simple tax' that it was once described as. However, when businesses have managed to find out how the various aspects of the tax affect them, they should be able to apply it without facing too many on-going difficulties. Checks are made from time to time by officers from the local VAT offices (LVOs); in this way Customs and Excise are able to ensure that no errors or mistakes are being made and that the correct amount of tax – not too much nor too little – is received into the Revenue coffers.

There is a network of LVOs throughout the country and you can find the address of yours in the telephone directory under Customs and Excise. If it does not have its own Advice Centre for dealing with everyday enquiries, you will be given the address and telephone number of the office which will handle calls from businesses in your area. It is always advisable to obtain answers in writing to any questions of a technical nature.

The following paragraphs give those who are new to the tax, or who have little experience of it, an insight into some of the rules and more common problems. Also mentioned are the procedures introduced by Customs to help ease the VAT burden for smaller businesses.

Rates of tax

The majority of goods and services supplied in the UK are liable to VAT at the standard rate of 17.5%. The rate for domestic fuel and power is 5%. These rates are termed 'positive' rates for VAT purposes. Most goods sent abroad, books and newspapers and foods sold in shops are, however, zero rated. Some services in connection with education, health, banking and insurance are exempt from VAT. It is important to realize that zero, as well as 5% and 17.5%, is a rate of tax since the time for deciding whether, and if so when, to register for VAT depends on the amount of taxable supplies made by your business. The turnover from any exempt supplies does not count towards the registration limit.

Registration

If your business is just starting, it is unlikely that you will have to register immediately: only when the value of your taxable supplies reaches £49,000 in a 'rolling' period of 12 months is application compulsory. Before 1 December 1997 the limit was £48,000.

It is vital that you do not delay submitting an application for registration as soon as it has to be made. Your LVO will arrange for the issue of a VAT 1 Form to you. This has to be completed no later than 30 days from the end of the month after the one in which your turnover exceeds the £49,000 limit.

Illustration

Simon Potter commenced in business on I May 1997. His turnover in what would be taxable supplies between May 1997 and June 1998 was as follows:

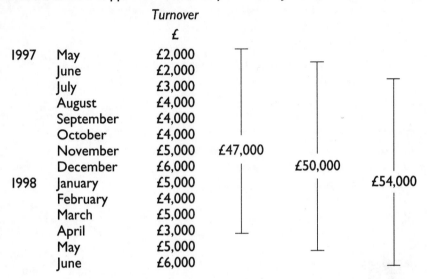

		Turnover £			
1997	May	£2,000			
	June	£2,000			
	July	£3,000			
	August	£4,000			
	September	£4,000			
	October	£4,000			
	November	£5,000	£47,000		
	December	£6,000		£50,000	
1998	January	£5,000			£54,000
	February	£4,000			
	March	£5,000			
	April	£3,000			
	May	£5,000			
	June	£6,000			

As the turnover in the period from 1 May 1997 to 30 April 1998 was less than £49,000, there was then no requirement to register. The 12 month period from 1 June 1997 to 31 May 1998 saw the turnover increase to £50,000. The VAT office should be advised during June 1998. Registration would usually be effective from 1 July 1998. Had the turnover in May 1998 remained at the same level as April the total turnover for the 'rolling' period of 12 months from the beginning of June 1997 to the end of May 1998 would have remained below the limit requiring registration. However, even if the May 1998 turnover figure was only £3,000, a June 1998 turnover of more than the same amount would take the total turnover for the 12 months ending 30 June 1998 above the compulsory limit.

Registration cannot be avoided unless Customs can be convinced that either

- a drop in turnover would mean that, from then on, it would remain at an annual level of less than £47,000, or

- the business would be one where, when registered, repayments of VAT would normally have to be made.

Requests not to be registered would, in these circumstances, normally be granted, providing the LVO was told of any changes which might alter the position.

Sometimes there are benefits in registering even though turnover does not come up to the compulsory registration limit. Voluntary registrations of this nature are allowed providing that you are, or will be, making some taxable supplies. In this way VAT incurred on your business expenses may be claimed back, including the VAT paid on assets like computers and printers on hand at the time of registration, as well as on certain business start-up costs.

If you are in partnership you must also complete a VAT 2 Form in addition to the VAT 1 Form.

Do not delay registering if you happen to buy an existing business, such as a shop, where the previous owner was already registered. The turnover build-up to £49,000 from the time you take on the business does not then apply. Sometimes it is possible for the registration number of the previous owner to be transferred to you.

Shortly after you have completed the registration forms and sent them off, you will receive a letter advising you of your registration number and a selection of notices and leaflets. Your formal certificate of registration will follow soon afterwards. The notices and leaflets will be of a general nature intended to help you understand the workings of the tax and to assist you in complying with all the rules and regulations. It may be that other leaflets are available which apply to your particular type of business and it is wise to ask your LVO to send these to you. A list of the leaflets most likely to be of help is in Table 4 at the end of the book.

New businesses which do not keep an eye on how their turnover is progressing can be caught out by a scaled penalty imposed for not registering when they should. The penalty is calculated as follows:

Registration not more than 9 months late	5%
Registration over 9 months but not more than 18 months late	10%
Registration more than 18 months late	15%

The penalty is based on the tax due for the period from the time registration should have started to the date the VAT 1 form is received by Customs or liability to be registered is discovered. There is a minimum penalty of £50.

A video on VAT is available free of charge on request and seminars are often arranged by the LVOs for newly registered businesses. If you receive an invitation to attend one, I suggest you take up the offer as it gives you an opportunity to get any points of doubt or difficulty cleared up.

Records and accounting

Output tax is what you are liable for on the supplies you make (outputs) and input tax is on the purchases you receive (inputs). You should keep a copy of every invoice issued for supplies made by your business. Normally, an analysed listing should be made of them showing the following:

Invoice		Customer	VAT excl Value	VAT	Gross Value	Date payment received
No	Date					
			£	£	£	

Similarly, purchase invoices should be analysed in your records and filed by you in such a way that it is possible to trace any item where input tax is claimed to the tax invoice for the purchase. Special care should be taken to make sure tax invoices do not get lost.

Whether or not you are able, or choose, to use Cash Accounting (see the section *Helpful schemes for smaller businesses* later on in the chapter), you will find it best to total your outputs and inputs monthly. You will then be well prepared to bring together the details for the VAT accounting periods shown on your certificate of registration. A summary of the monthly tax totals can be noted in a VAT Account which acts as a link between your own records and the VAT Return – Form VAT 100 – which will be sent to you. Very simply, and if you happen to be allocated quarters in line with the calendar quarters, the VAT Account may, for the January to March period, be like this:

VAT Account Period I January 1998 to 31 March 1998

	£	£
Output Tax		
January	2,470	
February	2,360	
March	2,520	
Total	£7,350	7,350

Input Tax

January	910	
February	820	
March	680	
	‾‾‾‾	
Total	£2,410	2,410
	═══	‾‾‾‾
Net amount due		£4,940
		═══

Using the figures in your VAT Account and the tax-exclusive values of your outputs and inputs you will be in a position to complete the various boxes on your VAT Return.

When the Return ends up showing an amount of tax due to the Customs and Excise you should send it off and pay what is due. If the VAT claimable on the purchases for the business exceeds the VAT charged on your supplies, the Return will show you are entitled to a repayment. It is likely this will be sent direct to your account although it may be subject to verification by your LVO before you receive the refund.

Input tax

It is only the input tax which is incurred on purchases for your business which can count towards how much is claimed. Sometimes you might incur expenses where the input tax cannot be claimed at all. Examples are business entertaining and private purchases paid for by your business. Occasionally there may be a need to apportion input tax such as that on home telephone bills, which are partly for business and partly for private purposes. Apportionment is best done on a percentage basis. Customs and Excise will go along with your method provided that it is reasonable.

Motor cars and fuel

Seldom are those businesses which are not directly concerned with motoring (that is those which are not like new car dealers, vehicle hirers, taxi drivers or driving schools) able to claim back all the input tax on cars which they buy or lease. Most cannot claim anything at all on cars they buy. With new car leases, however, it is now possible to claim 50% of the input tax on the rental payments.

As for motor fuel, there are two basic ways for dealing with input tax. All input tax on the fuel can be claimed with a fixed scale charge applied to take account of private use. Alternatively, no input tax is claimed and the fixed scale charge is ignored. As a guide the fixed scale charge is normally the better way if private motoring paid for by the business is more than about 8,000 miles a year.

The quarterly scale charges are as follows:

Engine Size – cc	Diesel		Petrol	
	Scale Charge	VAT	Scale Charge	VAT
	£	£	£	£
1400 or less	185	27.55	200	29.78
1401 to 1999	185	27.55	252	37.53
Over 1999	235	35.00	372	55.40

Input tax on repairs and maintenance of business cars can be claimed whichever way you decide to deal with motor fuel.

Special schemes for retailers

Retailers ofter sell a mixture of both positive and zero-rated goods but do not know how much of each from day to day. When this happens they can use one of the schemes devised to help them work out their VAT liabilities. If your business falls into this category, you should study the leaflets telling you about the various schemes so that you do not pay too much tax.

Where retailers sell only goods which are liable to the standard rate of 17.5%, the amount of tax included in the gross takings for a period is $7/47$. Referred to as the 'VAT fraction', the basis for this calculation is as follows:

		£
Tax exclusive value	(say)	100.00
Add: VAT @ 17.5%		17.50
Tax inclusive price		£117.50

The VAT included in the tax inclusive price is therefore:

$$\frac{17.5}{117.5} = \frac{7}{47}$$

For goods liable at 5% the 'VAT fraction' will be $1/21$. When retailers are asked for one, they must issue a proper tax invoice for supplies where the value exceeds £100. For supplies below this figure, till receipts will usually have enough information on them for the appropriate VAT fraction to be applied by customers who, in the course of their business, make retail purchases and want to claim back the input tax suffered.

Second-hand goods schemes

For many years there have been a number of schemes where certain types of business have had to keep detailed stock records. Using the 'VAT fraction' they have had to work out the tax to pay on an item-by-item basis according to how much the selling price exceeded the purchase price. In this way, the liability is just on the dealer's margin. These schemes continue to be available, but a Global Accounting Scheme now makes it much easier for those businesses which trade in large volumes of second-hand low-value goods to work out the tax. Although a values limit of £500 for an article has been set, a business which uses this scheme can take the overall margin in the whole of the tax period and apply the VAT fraction to it. An item by item calculation is unnecessary.

Helpful schemes for smaller businesses

Customs have moved a long way to bring in measures which ease the VAT accounting burden for smaller businesses. Those with an annual taxable turnover below £350,000 can operate Cash Accounting which means that output tax is worked out just on what is actually received. Input tax is claimed when bills are paid. Any business with a taxable turnover less than £300,000 can, when it has been registered for a year, apply to join the Annual Accounting Scheme. Apart from only having to submit one VAT Return each year there are other benefits from annual accounting, including:

- fewer declarations, therefore fewer deadlines and less risk of penalties;

- a reduction of some paperwork during the year, with an extra month to complete the annual return; and

- fixed interim payments that provide an aid to cash flow planning.

Those businesses with a turnover below £100,000, and where the estimated tax for the year is likely to be less than £2,000, need pay no instalments as the year goes along. If, based on the year before, tax of more than £2,000 is likely to be payable for the year ahead, then three quarterly payments of 20% of the previous year's liability will be payable. For businesses with a turnover between £100,000 and £300,000 there will be monthly payments to be made under the scheme. Final settlement comes at the year-end when it is time to prepare the annual return.

Bad debts

From time to time there is concern when customers delay or fail to pay their bills. Retailers and businesses using Cash Accounting for VAT do not pay VAT on the supplies they make unless they are themselves paid. For others VAT has to be paid over to Customs in the VAT period when tax invoices are issued. Of course, this has an adverse effect upon cash flow.

However, it is now possible to reclaim the VAT when more than six months have passed from the time when invoices should have been settled. You have to write telling the customer who owes you the money what you are going to do and, since he has to adjust his own tax, this may prompt him into settling your invoice. If he does not pay you, and you go ahead and claim the VAT included in the outstanding invoice, care has to be taken to make sure that the VAT fraction is applied to anything which is received later on. This has to be declared by being included with other output tax on the VAT Return for the period of receipt.

Partial exemption

This is a complex area which occurs when some supplies made by a business are taxable, whether at a positive or the zero rate, and others are exempt. Strictly, the input tax may only be claimed when it relates to taxable supplies, but this is not always so. A relaxation in the rules allows recovery of all claimable input tax if that which relates to the exempt supplies is less than both £625 per month on average and 50% of the total input tax. The calculations for this have to be done when each VAT Return is completed. An annual adjustment is then carried out to iron out any peaks and troughs which occurred during the year.

Routine control by the LVO

Every now and then your LVO will contact you. It may just be to ask you to send them a copy of the most recent annual accounts which have been prepared for your business. Alternatively it will be to arrange a visit to come along and see you. Initially, the officer will want a discussion with you and to ask questions about your business. This is followed by an examination of your books and records to make sure that you are keeping proper records and correctly dealing with your VAT Returns. The officer will draw your attention to any mistakes which he finds you have made and issue an assessment for any underdeclared or overdeclared tax. Since assessments may span the three years prior to the visit, it is worthwhile reviewing beforehand, as a precautionary measure, the Returns which you have submitted. Misdeclaration penalties and default interest may be imposed if substantial amounts of tax are found to have been underdeclared.

Penalties, surcharges and interest

There are a number of penalties for the unwary and non-compliant trader. Whenever Returns are submitted, the aim should be for the true tax in each and every period to be declared and paid. Getting it right first time is best for everybody's sake. Errors, although they may be innocent, are always possible. If, when you are preparing a Return for a current period, you find that you have made mistakes in preceding quarters, you may be able to make an appropriate adjustment without incurring a penalty.

Any errors which, taken altogether, involve an amount of tax less than £2,000 can be adjusted in the Return for a current quarter. However, if the total of any errors exceeds £2,000, spotting where they have been made and what they amount to, and owning up, means that the chance of incurring the misdeclaration penalty may be avoided. Form VAT 652 is available for notifying your VAT office of errors greater than £2,000. Alternatively, details of any errors of this size may be set out in a letter which should be sent together with a payment to correct the overall position. Default interest will normally be charged when assessments for errors are issued.

At the present time the level of the misdeclaration penalty is a flat 15% but whether or not it is imposed depends very much upon the correct amounts of output and input tax which should have been declared for the period.

Failure to pay the proper amount of tax when it is due can lead to the imposition of surcharges. These can range from 2% to 15% if a history of default builds up. Surcharge assessments will, however, seldom be issued unless calculated to exceed £200.

A further type of penalty may also apply if mistakes are persistently made.

Supplies to/from EU countries

There are special rules for these supplies which although they may differ from rules covering exports to, and imports from, countries outside the EU, have been designed to ease the difficulties which businesses have had to face in the past. It is as well to study carefully the appropriate leaflets issued by Customs if your business is likely to be involved with such trade.

Appeals

If you disagree with an officer's assessment or wish to appeal against a penalty or surcharge, you can ask for the matter to be reconsidered by your local VAT office. A review should be carried out by someone other than the officer who issued the assessment or penalty. Alternatively, an appeal can be lodged for hearing before an independent VAT Tribunal.

The outcome of appeals depends very much upon the reasons why mistakes were made in the first place. Innocence is not normally accepted as an excuse.

Complaints

Standards have to be laid down and all Customs officers are expected to abide by them. If ever you feel dissatisfied with the way our business affairs have been handled or that an officer has overstepped the mark and exceeded his authority, you should write in the first place to the Assistant Collector who is the head of your LVO. Failure to resolve complaints made locally can be followed up by contacting the Adjudicator's Office which is the independent body set up specifically for this purpose.

7

THE SELF-EMPLOYED

You cannot simply choose to be taxed as a self-employed person. It is a matter of fact whether you are working on your own account. The concept of self-employment extends to all trades, professions and vocations. You are not self-employed if you are running your business through a company. If you are employed but have some other freelance business activity as well, you will be taxed on these profits as a self-employed person.

The obligations imposed on the taxpayer who is self-employed are more onerous than those which apply to the employee. Proper records must be maintained of all business transactions. At the end of each financial year they are all brought together into an account of the income and expenditure of the business. Whenever possible a balance sheet should be drawn up showing the assets and liabilities of the business at the year end.

Records
Self-Assessment brings with it a new requirement for keeping records. The records you should maintain will depend upon the type and size of your business. You are, however, expected to record all of the following:

- sales and other business receipts as they come in, and you should retain the back-up records (for example, invoices, bank statements and paying-in slips to show where the income came from);

- purchases and other expenses for which, wherever possible, you should retain invoices for the goods acquired or costs incurred;

- purchases and sales of assets used in your business;

- amounts taken out of the business for personal use (drawings) and all monies paid into your business from personal funds (capital introduced).

For most businesses it is also good practice to maintain a separate bank account for the business and keep the following books of account:

- a cash book which summarizes and analyses all the entries in the bank account;

- a petty cash book to record all small cash transactions.

If you run a larger business you may well need to keep other books of account as well. No matter how large or small your business you would be well advised to write up your books frequently.

You will have to retain your records for 5 years from the latest date by which your Tax Return has to be filed. For example, your completed Tax Return for the year to 5 April 1998 must be sent back to your tax office by no later than 31 January 1999. It follows that your records for that year must be retained until 31 January 2004.

Accounts

You can choose the date to which you make up the accounts of your trade or business each year. For this reason it is unlikely that the first accounts will cover a full year's business activities. Thereafter your accounts should continue to be made up to the same date every year although you can alter this where you can show good reason for a change.

Your accounts should be drawn up to show the profit or loss earned in the financial year. This is not usually the simple difference between the cash received and the cash paid out. For example, if you sell to some of your customers on credit there will inevitably be some unpaid invoices at the end of the financial year. Nevertheless, the amount of these outstanding invoices needs to come into your accounts as income for that period. Equally, where amounts are owing to your suppliers at the year-end these must be brought into the accounts as expenses incurred in the year. If your trade is one where you need to keep a stock of raw materials or finished goods, the value of that stock at the year-end must enter your accounts. It will usually be valued at cost or, in the case of redundant or old stock, at realizable value.

Make sure you include in your accounts all the expenses of running your business. If, for example, you are a married man and your wife helps you by taking telephone messages or acting as your part-time assistant or secretary, pay her a proper wage for these services. What you pay her can count as an expense in your accounts. She can then set off her personal allowance against her wages. If these are less than £3,224 a year there will be no tax or National Insurance to pay on them. There will be some items of expenditure, such as a car used both privately and in your business, when it will be difficult to differentiate precisely between the private and business elements of the expenditure. Where there is this overlap you should agree the proportion which relates to your business with the Inland Revenue. If you do your office work from home you can include as a deduction in your accounts a proportion of your home expenses, such as light, heat and insurance. Remember that if part of your home is used exclusively for business purposes, then should you come to sell your house the profit on sale attributable to that part will not be exempt from Capital Gains Tax.

Illustration

David Smith runs a successful art gallery from rented high street premises. He employs a full-time assistant. His wife keeps his accounts and does his VAT returns as well as acting as part-time secretary.

David started up in business in May 1994. He makes up his account to 31 December each year. The statement of his business income and expenses for the financial year to 31 December 1997 is as follows:

David Smith
Art Gallery

Profit and Loss Account for the year ended 31 December 1997

		£
Sales		116,250
Less: Cost of sales		
Stock of pictures at start of year	6,800	
Purchases during the year	62,400	
	69,200	
Less: Stock of pictures at end of year	7,700	
		61,500
Gross Profit		54,750
Less: Overhead expenses		

		£	
Gallery expenses			
Rent and rates		9,500	
Light and heat		670	
Telephone		420	
Insurance		230	
Redecorations		1,200	
			12,020
Assistant's salary and pension contribution			12,050
Wife's salary			3,100
Postage and stationery			180
Advertising			340
Travelling			460
Entertaining			220
Trade books and magazines			110
Trade subscription			140
Car expenses			
Road Fund Licence			
and Insurance		380	
Petrol and oil		650	
Repairs and servicing		120	
		1,150	
Business proportion	75%		862
Use of home as office	($1/7 \times 560$)		80
Home telephone	(25%)		90
Overdraft interest			720
Provision for bad debts	($10\% \times 2,500$)		250
Donations to charity	(non-business)		60
Miscellaneous expenses			108
			30,790
Profit for the year			£23,960

Standard accounting information

If at any time during the 1997/98 tax year you were in business then you will need to fill in the self-employment pages of your Tax Return for that year. For those in business with a turnover of more than £15,000 there is now a set format, as part of the self-employment pages of the Return, for reporting the annual income and expenses of your business. If accounts are not presented in the required format the Return will not be accepted as complete.

Illustration

When David Smith, the art gallery proprietor, comes to complete the self-employment pages of his Tax Return for the year ended 5 April 1998 he will fill in the section on business income and expenses for his financial year to 31 December 1997 as follows:

	£	£
Sales/business income (excluding VAT)		116,250
Less: Cost of sales	61,500	
Other direct costs	–	
	———	61,500
Gross profit		54,750
Other income/profits		–
		54,750
Less: Expenses		
Employee costs	15,150	
Premises costs	10,480	
Repairs	1,200	
General administrative expenses	940	
Motor expenses	862	
Travel and subsistence	460	
Advertising, promotion and entertainment	560	
Legal and professional costs	–	
Bad debts	250	
Interest	720	
Other finance charges	–	
Depreciation and loss/(profit) on sale	–	
Other expenses	168	
Total expenses		30,790
Net profit		£23,960

Notes:– £

(1) Employee costs are:

	£
Assistant's salary	12,050
Wife's salary	3,100
	£15,150

(2) Premises costs are:

	£
Gallery – rent and rates	9,500
– light and heat	670
– insurance	230
Use of home as office	80
	£10,480

(3) General administrative expenses are:

	£
Postage and stationery	180
Telephone (gallery and home)	510
Trade books and magazines	110
Trade subscription	140
	£940

(4) Other expenses are:

	£
Miscellaneous expenses	108
Donations to charity	60
	£168

In order to minimize the risk of an Inland Revenue enquiry into your business accounts and Tax Return, it is important that the analysis of your business expenses over the various headings in the standardized accounting format follows a consistent pattern from year to year.

If the total annual turnover of your business is below £15,000 you can fill in the special, shortened income and expenses section in the self-employment pages of the Return. This comprises a three line statement of:

• turnover and other business receipts;

• business expenses allowable for tax;

• resulting profit or loss.

You should, of course, still keep proper business accounts and records in order that you can draw up the annual three-line statement accurately.

Adjustment of profits

It does not follow that the profit shown by your business accounts is the same as the one on which you pay tax. This is because some items of expenditure are specifically not deductible in computing your taxable business profits. Types of expenditure which come into this category are business entertainment, non-business charitable donations, general provisions and reserves, professional costs related to capital expenditure, and the cost of items of a capital, as opposed to revenue, nature.

Illustration

Although David Smith's accounts for his financial year to 31 December 1997 show a profit of £23,960, his taxable profits are £24,490, as follows:

	£	£
Profit as per accounts		23,960
Add Disallowable expenses:		
General provision for bad debts	250	
Entertainment	220	
Donations	60	
		530
Profit as adjusted for tax purposes		£24,490

The current-year basis of taxation

Under the current-year basis of taxation, self-employed individuals are taxed on the profits made in the tax year. The profits shown by annual accounts drawn up to a date other than the end of the tax year – 'the basis period' – are regarded as those of the year to 5 April.

Illustration

The tax-adjusted profit of £24,490 of David Smith's art gallery business for the year to 31 December 1997 will be taxed in 1997/98.

For the first year of business the taxable profits will be limited to those arising in the period from commencement to 5 April. On cessation the profits for the final tax year will be those arising in the period from the end of the basis period taxed in the previous tax year.

Under these rules it is possible that some periods of account will feature for more than one tax year. However, over the lifetime of a business it is intended that the profits should be taxed in full, once and once only. Accordingly, any profits which are taxed more than once will be eligible for a special relief. Known as overlap relief, it will be given either when a business ceases or for any earlier tax year for which the basis period is longer than 12 months.

Illustration

James Gray started his business on 1 August 1997. His annual accounting date is 31 July. He makes the following profits:

Year to 31.07.1998	£15,000
Year to 31.07.1999	£18,000

The taxable profits for the first three tax years are:

Tax Year	Basis Period	Taxable Profit
		£
1997/98	01.08.1997 to 05.04.1998	10,000
1998/99	Year to 31.07.1998	15,000
1999/2000	Year to 31.07.1999	18,000

The business closes down on 30 April 2005. The taxable profit in the final period from 1 August 2004 to 30 April 2005 amounts to £12,000. The final tax year is 2005/06 when James will be taxable on:

		£
Taxable profit in final period		12,000
Less: Overlap	01.08.1997 to 05.04.1998	10,000
Net taxable amount		£2,000

Special rules apply when a business changes its accounting date. Apart from the first and last years of business the system aims to tax the profits of a 12-month period in each tax year.

Illustration

Sheila Windows commenced her business on 1 November 1997. She draws up her first accounts to 31 October 1998 which disclose a profit of £15,000. She then changes her accounting date to 31 December 1999. The accounts for the 14-month period show a taxable profit of £14,000. Her basis periods and taxable profits for the opening years of assessment are:

Tax Year	Basis Period	Taxable Profit
		£
1997/98	01.11.1997 to 05.04.1998	6,250
1998/99	Year to 31.10.1998	15,000

The overlap period is from 01.11.1997 to 05.04.1998:

1999/2000	01.11.1998 to 31.12.1999	
	(14 months)	14,000
Less: Overlap	01.11.1997 to 31.12.1997	2,500
Net taxable amount		£11,500

The overlap period was one of five months. As the accounting period from 1 November 1998 to 31 December 1999 is 14 months, the overlap relief is two months. The amount deducted from the assessment for 1999/2000 is $2/5$ of the original overlap profit. Three months of overlap relief is then available either when the business ceases or for any subsequent tax year when the basis period is longer than 12 months.

Post-cessation expenses

Tax relief is allowed on specific types of expense incurred after a business has ceased. Relief is available for payments made within 7 years of the permanent discontinuance of the business. The types of expense which qualify for this form of relief are those closely related to the trading or professional activities while they were carried on. Included, for example, is relief for debts which subsequently proved to be irrecoverable.

The relief is given by setting the payments made against income for the same tax year. Any excess can be treated as a capital loss of the same year only. Any unrelieved post-cessation expenses cannot be carried back or forward against either income or capital gains.

Capital allowances

Although you cannot deduct expenditure on items of a capital nature directly from your business profits, you do receive what are known as capital allowances on the expenditure. Amounts spent on machinery, equipment, motor vans, fixtures and fittings, and motor cars qualify for a writing-down allowance of 25% per annum, commencing with the year of purchase. Thereafter the annual allowance of 25% is calculated on the balance after deduction of previous allowances. For cars costing more than £12,000 there is a maximum allowance of £3,000 per annum.

Expenditure on plant and machinery, but not motor cars, incurred by small- and medium-sized businesses (your business is almost certain to qualify) in the 12 months to 1 July 1998 attracts a 50% first-year allowance. This allowance is given instead of the 25% writing down allowance otherwise available in the year when expenditure is incurred. The balance of expenditure will continue to be written down in subsequent years on the reducing balance basis at the rate of 25% per annum.

A separate 'pool' of expenditure must be maintained for each of the following different categories:

- plant and equipment, including motor vans and lorries;

- cars costing up to £12,000;

- each car bought for over £12,000;

- each asset used for both personal and business use;

- each asset with a short life expectancy.

Where an asset on which capital allowances have been given is sold, the proceeds of sale must come into the computation of capital allowances. This can sometimes lead to a further allowance where an asset is sold for less than its written-down value for tax purposes. Alternatively, if it fetches an amount greater than its written-down value this can often mean that part of the allowances already given need to be withdrawn. These adjustments are respectively referred to as balancing allowances and balancing charges.

Illustration

In his accounting year to 31 December 1997, our art gallery proprietor, David Smith, traded in his old car for £1,500 and bought a new car for £10,800. In October of the year he also spent £1,200 on a desk and chairs. His claim to capital allowances for 1997/98, based on his capital expenditure in the year to 31 December 1997, is:

		Pool £	Car with Private Use £
Written-down values brought forward from 1996/97		800	1,800
Sale proceeds of car			1,500
Balancing allowance			300
Additions in the year:			
Desk and chairs		1,200	
New car			10,800
		2,000	
Allowances due:			
First year – 50%	600		800
Writing down – 25%	200	800	2,700
Carried forward to 1998/99		£1,200	£8,100

Summary of allowances:

First year	600
Writing down	2,900
Balancing	300
	3,800
Less: 25% private use of car	750
1997/98 Capital allowances	£3,050

Capital allowances are treated as a trading expense of your business. Any balancing charges are added to your profit as a trading receipt. It follows that the chargeable period for the purposes of calculating your capital allowances is the same as that for which you draw up your accounts. This means that the amount of writing-down allowances to which you are entitled is determined by reference to the length of the period of account. Thus, if you draw up accounts for an 8-month period, $8/12$ of the writing-down allowances can be set against taxable profits for that period. Similarly, if a period of account extends to 15 months the tax deductible allowances are equivalent to $15/12$ of the writing-down allowances. In the event that a period of account exceeds 18 months it will be divided into one of 12 months and the balancing period with a restricted writing-down allowance.

Under Self-Assessment there is a section in the self-employment pages of your Tax Return for you to summarize your claim to capital allowances.

Losses

Most businesses cannot escape going through a bad spell at some stage in their existence. Where the results of the business for the year show a loss you will be able to claim tax relief on the loss as increased by any claim to capital allowances which now count as trading expenses. You can elect to set a trading loss against other income for the same tax year, or the preceding year. You cannot claim relief for only part of a loss.

Illustration

Martin Peters has been in business for many years. He makes up his accounts to 30 November each year. He makes a loss in the year ended 30 November 1999 which can be claimed against his other income in 1999/2000 and/or carried back and relieved against his total income in 1998/99.

Any unrelieved loss of your business must then be carried forward to be set against the profits from the same business in later years.

Otherwise you can claim to offset a trading loss against capital gains.

The claim is for relief on the amount of the trading loss which cannot be set against your other income in the year or on which tax relief has already been allowed in some other way. The maximum loss eligible for relief against capital gains is equivalent to the amount on which you would be chargeable to Capital Gains Tax before deducting the annual exemption limit (see Chapter 13). It is not possible to make a partial claim. As a result, it is possible that personal allowances may be wasted as well as the annual exemption for Capital Gains Tax.

There is an alternative form of loss relief available for new businesses. It allows losses incurred during the first four years of assessment to be set against your income in the three years prior to that in which the loss arises. Relief is first of all given against your income for the earliest year. For example, if you started out in business during 1997/98 and incur a loss in the first period of trading, the proportion attributable to the tax year 1997/98 can be set off against your income in 1994/95, 1995/96 and 1996/97, starting with 1994/95.

Frequently it is necessary to incur expenditure on a new business venture before it starts to trade. Any such expenditure incurred within seven years prior to the commencement of trade is treated as a separate loss sustained in the tax year in which trading began.

There is also a special form of loss relief for those businesses which incur a loss in their final period of trading. As the business has ceased there cannot be any future profits against which the loss might be relieved. Therefore, you are allowed to set a loss arising in the last 12 months of trading against the profits from the same business in the final tax year as well as the three preceding years, beginning with the profits of the last year and working backwards.

Illustration

Ralph Collins retires from business on 30 November 1998. Apart from the final 8 months when he loses £21,000 his business had always been successful. His profits and the assessments based on these were as follows:

Accounting Year	Taxable Profits	Year of Assessment
	£	
Year ended 31 March 1994	17,000	1994/95
" " " 1995	15,000	1995/96
2 years " " " 1997	6,000 (50%)	1996/97
Year ended " " 1998	8,000	1997/98

The terminal loss can be set off as follows:

1997/98	8,000	leaving nil taxable profits
1996/97	6,000	leaving nil taxable profits
1995/96	7,000	reducing the taxable profits to £8,000

£21,000

The Enterprise Allowance

The Enterprise Allowance is a weekly payment for one year to individuals leaving the unemployment register to set up in business. The allowance is not included in the takings of the recipient's business, although it is chargeable to Income Tax.

Business Economic Notes

Business Economic Notes are published from time to time by the Inland Revenue. They give information on the finance and business background of particular trades and professions and are used in tax offices when traders' business accounts are examined. The notes are based primarily on research into publicly available material such as the trade press and specialist books of reference. They have also been discussed with some or all of the principal trade and professional associations. However, they are not intended to be definitive or comprehensive descriptions of particular trades or professions. The Business Economic Notes published so far are listed in Table 4 at the end of the book, and can be obtained from the Inland Revenue Reference Room, at Somerset House in London. There is a small fee to pay.

Special situations

In the space available it has only been possible for me to paint a general picture of the way in which business profits are taxed. If you are a Lloyds underwriter, a farmer, a writer or a subcontractor in the construction industry you should be aware that there are special rules which apply in calculating the tax on the profits from your trade or profession. In these and other situations it is advisable to seek professional assistance.

The letting of holiday accommodation in the UK is treated as a trade. The accommodation has to be furnished residential property which is available for renting by the public as holiday accommodation for at least 140 days during each tax year. It must actually be let for a minimum of 70 days. There are other requirements which also need to be satisfied. Capital gains on disposals of holiday accommodation falling within these rules qualify for the replacement and retirement reliefs which apply to business assets as well as the new re-investment relief (see Chapter 13)

8

NATIONAL INSURANCE CONTRIBUTIONS, STATE SOCIAL SECURITY AND INSURED BENEFITS

Whether you are employed or self-employed, you will have to pay National Insurance Contributions, as well as Income Tax, on your earnings or business profits. In turn, the payment of sufficient National Insurance Contributions on your earnings makes you eligible to claim those Social Security benefits which are based on your contribution history. Some benefits, however, such as Child Benefit, do not depend upon the payment of contributions.

It is the Department of Social Security (DSS) which is responsible for administering all aspects of the Social Security system. There are local DSS offices throughout the country. The framework of the Social Security system is now so substantial, and the range of benefits so wide and varied, it is only possible for me to give a brief summary of the system of contributions and benefits.

National Insurance Contributions

There are four different types of contribution which are payable:

- Class 1 by employees;

- Class 2 by the self-employed;

- Class 3 which is voluntary;

- Class 4 by the self-employed based on profits.

You will not be liable for contributions once you have retired and passed normal retirement age, which is 60 for a woman and 65 for a man, even if you carry on working for someone else or in your own business.

For National Insurance the earnings of employees on which Class 1 contributions are calculated include:

- a salary or wage – before deduction for pension contributions;

- holiday and sick pay;

- tax-free earnings from an employer's Profit Related Pay scheme.

However, no contributions are payable on benefits-in-kind.

Your contributions are usually worked out as a percentage of your weekly salary or wage. Nowadays however, many employees are paid less frequently – usually every month – when their contributions will be calculated by reference to the corresponding monthly lower and upper earnings limits. If you choose to have a break when moving jobs, or there is a period when you are unemployed, this has no effect on the contributions you will have to pay when you go back to work.

There are special rules for company directors. The contributions due from a company director are usually worked out on the assumption that the remuneration paid is attributable to an annual earnings period.

If you have more than one employment you are liable for contributions on your earnings from all your employers. Nevertheless there is an overall annual maximum limit of contributions payable by employees. Where the total amount of deductions for your National Insurance Contributions exceeds this annual limit then you should apply for a refund of the overpayment. Alternatively you can apply for deferment where you can envisage that the contributions which will be taken off your earnings from two or more employments are such that the total deductions will exceed the maximum annual limit. To apply for deferment you will need to complete a form CF379 before the beginning of the tax year when you want to defer the payment of contributions. The DSS will then instruct one or other of your employers not to withhold contributions from your earnings. After the end of the tax year your overall contribution history for that year is reviewed. If, for some reason or another, insufficient contributions have been collected on the earnings from all employments then the DSS will send you a calculation and demand for the balance due.

There are two rates of National Insurance Contributions payable by the self-employed. Class 2 is a weekly flat rate. You can pay by either direct debit every month or by quarterly bill every 13 weeks. If your earnings are below a specified annual limit you can be exempted from paying these contributions. You should apply in advance for small-earnings exception. Class 4 contributions are based on a percentage of your taxable business profits, after capital allowances, but before relief for pension contributions. These are accounted for through the tax system along with the annual tax liability on your profits as a self-employed taxpayer.

In certain circumstances, for example where you are also in employment and paying Class 1 contributions, you can apply to defer payment of both Class 2 and Class 4 contributions.

The payment of Class 3 contributions is voluntary. An individual who is neither employed nor in self-employment can pay Class 3 contributions in order to preserve entitlement to the state pension on retirement.

The rates of National Insurance Contributions for 1997/98 are in Table 5 at the end of the book. Like the Inland Revenue, the DSS publishes many helpful explanatory pamphlets. These can be obtained from your local Social Security office. Table 6 is a list of those leaflets with the widest application.

State Retirement Pensions

There are three types of state retirement pension:

- the basic retirement (or old person's) pension;

- a state earnings related pension (SERPS);

- a graduated pension.

State retirement pensions are payable to men who have reached age 65 and to women aged 60, subject, of course, to their contribution history. The contribution requirements which you must meet before you are entitled to the basic state pension are:

- The payment of

  - 50 flat-rate contributions at any time before 6 April 1975 or

  - Class 1, 2 or 3 National Insurance Contributions in any one tax year since 6 April 1975 such as to make that year a qualifying year. This is one in which you have received qualifying earnings equivalent to at least 52 times the lower earnings limit for National Insurance purposes for that year.

- The establishment of qualifying years for around 90% of your working life before you can receive the full basic pension. You need 9 or 10 qualifying years to get the minimum – 25% – basic pension payable.

As the name implies, the state earnings-related pension scheme (SERPS) is dependent on your earnings. You can get this additional pension if in any tax year since April 1978 you have paid the standard rate of Class 1 National Insurance Contributions on earnings between the lower and upper earnings limits. Furthermore, each Class 2 Contribution paid by the self-employed counts as one week's earnings at the lower earnings limit applying in that year.

As well as being entitled to the basic and additional pensions, certain individuals will be entitled to a pension under the graduated scheme. This was in operation between April 1961 and April 1975.

In addition to the basic pension a man may receive extra pension for:

- a wife;

- dependent children;

- a woman looking after his children.

A married woman may benefit from a retirement pension in one or other of three distinct ways:

- on her own contribution record;

- based on her husband's contribution if she is over 60 and retired so long as her husband is receiving a basic retirement pension;

- as a wife dependent on her husband. He is then entitled to an increase in his pension.

The retirement pension payable to a widow will depend on whether she was widowed before the normal retirement age of 60 or was widowed afterwards.

Social Security Benefits

Many benefits are only payable to individuals who have an established history of paying National Insurance Contributions. The type of benefit you can then claim depends on the nature of contributions paid as follows:

Type of Benefit	Class 1 (Employed)	Class 2 (Self-Employed)	Class 3 (Voluntary)
Retirement Pension			
– basic	Yes	Yes	Yes
– additional	Yes	No	No
Widow's pension	Yes	Yes	Yes
Widow's payment	Yes	Yes	Yes
Widowed mother's allowance	Yes	Yes	Yes
Maternity allowance	Yes	Yes	No
Incapacity benefit	Yes	Yes	No
Jobseeker's allowance	Yes	No	No

Other benefits do not depend upon the payment of contributions. Equally some benefits paid to you by the state are taxable, others are tax free.

To be able to claim either statutory maternity or sick pay you must be earning enough to pay Class 1 National Insurance contributions. A woman will qualify for statutory maternity pay if she has been working for the same employer continuously for 26 weeks up to, and including, the 15th week before her baby is due. She must provide evidence of being pregnant and give her employer sufficient notice of leaving work. The benefit is payable for 18 weeks beginning not earlier than the 11th week before the baby is due although the woman can actually select the time over which she will be absent from work.

Statutory sick pay is a flat-rate cash payment made to employees by their employer. To be eligible to claim you must be both incapable of work and not actually do any work at all on the day in question. It is not payable for the first three agreed qualifying days in any period when you are too unwell to work. In any period of sickness you have a maximum entitlement to 28 weeks of statutory sick pay.

Incapacity benefit is a benefit for individuals under state pension age, provided they have paid a qualifying amount of National Insurance contributions, who are unable to work because of illness or disability. Employees will normally get statutory sick pay for the first 28 weeks of sickness before moving on to incapacity benefit at the short-term higher rate. There are three different rates of benefit and additional supplements which may be paid. Incapacity benefit is not means-tested, but it is taxable. Any tax due will be deducted directly from the benefit paid to claimants who do not have another source of income already subject to PAYE. Where claimants do have another source of income on which PAYE is applied – such as an occupational pension from a former employer – any tax due on the benefit will be collected by adjusting the tax code applied to the other income and deducting tax from that other income.

In order to claim the jobseeker's allowance an individual needs to satisfy a number of conditions. The main features of the jobseeker's allowance, which is taxable, are that:

- entitlement is based on either a satisfactory contribution record or a means-tested low income;

- it is a weekly benefit with supplements for age and other personal circumstances;

- it is payable to unemployed individuals between the ages of 18 and state pensionable age. A claimant must sign a jobseeker's agreement which sets out the steps he or she intends to take towards full-time employment.

An individual is disqualified from receiving benefit if he or she fails to honour the obligations of the jobseeker's agreement, or refuses to follow either recommendations or directions of the employment advisor.

Other benefits include:

- income support, which is a non-contributory weekly benefit paid to individuals who do not have sufficient money to live on. The needs of each claimant are assessed depending on their circumstances. However, claimants with savings and capital over £8,000 do not qualify for income support.

- child benefit, which is not means tested and is payable to individuals bringing up children. For couples who are married it is the wife who should make the claim. The benefit is payable for all children under 16 years old. Children over age 15, but under 19, still qualify providing they are still in full-time education which includes courses at school or college up to 'A' Level. Child benefit is not payable for children studying beyond this level – for example for a university degree.

- benefits for the disabled such as the attendance and invalid care allowances. The attendance allowance is targeted at individuals who are seriously disabled, mentally or physically, and who need a lot of care and attention. On the other hand the invalid care allowance is payable to those individuals who are unable to work because they have to look after a relative who is either sick or disabled.

All the Social Security benefits, distinguishing between those which are taxable and non-taxable, are listed in Table 7 at the end of the book. The rates of the main taxable Social Security benefits for 1997/98 are in Table 8.

Insured benefits

Benefits paid under insurance policies which provide against financial loss caused by unemployment, accident, sickness disability or infirmity are not taxable. The different types of insurance policy with tax-free benefits are:

- mortgage payment protection insurance: These provide income to meet mortgage commitments in the event of accident, sickness, disability or unemployment;

- permanent health insurance: These provide continuing income in the event of accident, sickness or disability;

- creditor insurance: These provide benefits to meet existing obligations and commitments, such as loans and domestic utility bills;

- certain kinds of long-term care insurance: that is those which provide benefits to meet the cost of the provision of care in the event of accident, sickness, disability or infirmity but only where policies are taken out before the need for care becomes apparent.

9

PERSONAL PENSIONS

Wherever possible I imagine you will want to avoid a drop in your living standards when you come to retire. When you can afford to do so, you should start contributing towards a pension to supplement the benefits you will receive from the State.

Many employers operate their own Company Pension Scheme. If you are in employment you will probably be able to join your employer's scheme. Some employers do not require their employees to make any contributions towards their benefits on retirement. In other cases employees must set aside varying percentages of their annual salary in addition to the amounts that their employers pay into their schemes each year. The maximum amount you can contribute is 15% of your salary. It is highly likely that your contributions will be much lower than this limit. You can use the remainder of your allowance by paying premiums into your own free-standing Additional Voluntary Contributions Scheme.

If your employer has not set up his own scheme for his employees or you are self-employed you will need to make your own pension arrangements. You will do this by taking out a Personal Pension Plan. These are generally available from Insurance Companies, Banks and Building Societies.

Eligible individuals
You can take out a personal pension plan if:

- you are self-employed;

- you are in employment. You can even choose to opt out of your employer's own company scheme and take out a personal pension plan instead. Your employer can make contributions into your personal pension plan in addition to the amount of premiums you choose to pay into the plan;

- you opt out of the state earnings-related pension scheme (SERPS). The Department of Social Security will then pay the difference between the full and reduced rates of National Insurance contributions into your personal pension scheme. Opting out of SERPS does not affect your entitlement to the basic State Pension.

Benefits on retirement
When you start making regular monthly or annual contributions into a personal pension plan do remember you cannot benefit from the funds building up in your plan until you come to retire and draw your pension.

Throughout this period your contributions will be invested in a tax-free fund. As we will see later on in this chapter you will also receive tax relief on your premiums. You benefit from a further tax concession on retirement when 25% of the value of the fund built up in your personal pension plan can be paid to you as a tax-free lump sum. The remainder of your fund is used to provide a pension which will be payable throughout the rest of your life. You can even arrange for this to be paid for a minimum guaranteed period, usually five years, should you die within this period. It is also possible to provide for a widow's pension if you die before your wife. As we will see in Chapter 11 the pension you eventually come to draw from your scheme is taxable.

The tax-free lump sum and pension can be taken at any time between the ages of 50 and 75. You do not actually need to retire before taking your pension. The Inland Revenue has approved earlier retirement ages of 30, 35, 40 or 45 for some professions and occupations, particularly in professional sport; for example, footballers can retire at age 35 and take maximum benefits. Those benefits within your plan which were purchased through opting out of SERPS cannot be drawn until you reach normal state retirement age.

If unfortunately you die before retirement a lump sum, depending on the terms of your particular plan, will probably be refundable. This can be paid out to beneficiaries nominated by you during your lifetime or, alternatively, to your executors. Any lump sum payable is free of tax.

Deferred annuities

Holders of personal pension plans can defer, if they wish, the purchase of their annuity up to age 75. In the meantime, during the deferral period, they can make income withdrawals taxable under PAYE in the same way as annuities. There is a set formula for working out the maximum amount of income withdrawal, which must be reviewed every three years.

During the period of deferral, the pension fund remains tax free and protected from Inheritance Tax. However, no further contributions can then be made into the plan.

Should the personal pension plan holder die after benefits have been taken from the plan, but before the annuity has been purchased, a surviving spouse or dependant has three options:

- for the time being to continue making income withdrawals. The annuity can be purchased either on the deceased's 75th birthday or his or her own 75th birthday, whichever is the earlier;

- to purchase an annuity immediately;

- to take the fund in cash, when there will be a special 35% tax charge on the value of the fund.

Tax relief on premiums

If you are in employment your premiums can be paid after deduction of tax at the basic rate. If you are liable to tax at the higher rate of 40%, you will need to tell your tax office about your personal pension plan so that the extra tax relief on your premiums over and above that due at the basic rate can be allowed in your code number. Your earnings for personal pension purposes include the annual amount of your taxable benefits-in-kind.

If you are self-employed, the premiums you pay are allowed as a deduction from your profits. For this purpose your earnings are your annual taxable business profits as reduced by capital allowances and any losses.

The most you can contribute each year is expressed as a percentage of your earnings and depends on your age. Furthermore, there is a maximum earnings limit on which the percentage limit can be calculated. For 1997/98 this is £84,000. It increases each year in line with the movement in the Retail Prices Index. The contribution limits are as follows:

Age at Start of Tax Year	Percentage Limit of Earnings
	%
Under 36	17½
36-45	20
46-50	25
51-55	30
56-60	35
Over 60	40

Up to 5% of your annual profits can be paid into a policy providing for the payment of a lump sum to your dependants in the event of your death before the age of 75. Premiums paid into such a policy count as part of the maximum permissible limits set out above.

Where you do not pay premiums up to the maximum permissible amount in any year the shortfall can be carried forward for up to six years. Relief outstanding for earlier years is used up before that still available for later years.

Illustration

Peter Wong has been in business for many years. Since 1993/94 Peter has not been making the maximum contributions towards his pension, as follows:

Tax Year	Premiums Paid	Maximum Permissible	Shortfall
	£	£	£
1993/94	1,000	2,200	1,200
1994/95	1,100	1,400	300
1995/96	1,100	1,500	400
1996/97	1,600	2,900	1,300

During 1997/98 Peter paid premiums of £4,500; the maximum permissible premium limit for the year was only £2,000. Nevertheless relief will be given for £4,500, as follows:

	£	£
Premium limit for 1997/98		2,000
Unused relief:		
1993/94	1,200	
1994/95	300	
1995/96	400	
1996/97 (part)	600	
		2,500
1997/98 Pension premium relief		£4,500

Premiums paid in the year can either be deducted from your taxable profits in the year of payment, or alternatively you can elect for them to be treated as if paid in the preceding year providing you do not exceed the contribution limit for the earlier year, including unused relief.

Unfortunately the carry-back rules do not fit in comfortably with Self-Assessment. The Inland Revenue does not want to revise self-assessments of earlier years arising out of elections to carry back personal pension premiums. Their stated approach on the tax relief due on a pension premium related back to the previous year is:

• It gives rise to a 'free-standing tax credit', based on the tax rates of the earlier year;

• which will be given to the taxpayer by 'repayment of offset';

• but which will not be repaid to the taxpayer until the tax liability for the earlier year has been paid.

Retirement annuities

Personal pension schemes have been around since the beginning of July 1988. Up to that date the self-employed and employees who were not members of their employer's own pension schemes could take out retirement annuities. No new retirement annuities may now be taken out although you can continue to pay regular and single premiums into existing contracts.

Retirement annuities differ from personal pension plans in a number of ways:

- employers are not allowed to make contributions into them;

- although there is no maximum earnings limit on which premiums may be paid, the contribution limits are not so generous:

Age at Start of Tax Year	Percentage Limit of Earnings %
Under 51	17½
51-55	20
56-60	22½
Over 60	27½

- you cannot draw your benefits before age 60. It is possible to transfer the benefits under a retirement annuity to a personal pension in order to draw down the tax-free lump sum and pension before age 60;

- you cannot use a retirement annuity to opt out of SERPS;

- if you are in employment you cannot pay your premiums after the deduction at source of tax at the basic rate;

- the method of calculating the maximum amount of the tax-free lump sum on retirement is more generous.

Waiver of premium benefits

For the payment of an additional premium within the overall percentage limits – typically between 2% and 3% of pension premiums – an individual can go a long way towards providing for the future security of his or her family. This extra premium also attracts tax relief at the individual's highest rate of tax.

In return the insurance company undertakes, in the event of ill health, to continue contributing to the individual's pension plan and to maintain full bonuses/benefits.

Personal pension planning

If you are still contributing into a retirement annuity you will often have to decide between continuing with this policy or instead opting to take out a personal pension plan. Where your salary or profits fall short of the earnings 'cap' of £84,000 you should consider contributing as much as you can into an existing retirement annuity as well as taking advantage of the higher contribution limits for personal pensions.

Illustration

John Wallace aged 44 earns £54,000 per annum. He has an existing retirement annuity and pays premiums of £5,200 each year.

John's maximum contribution limits are:

(1) Into his retirement annuity – £9,450 (17½% x £54,000)

(2) Into a personal pension – £10,800 (20% x £54,000)

John can pay either:

(a) A further £4,250 into his retirement annuity and contribute £1,350 into a personal pension, or

(b) A premium of £5,600 into a personal pension.

If you earn more than the amounts in the following table you should consider paying the maximum premiums into your retirement annuity.

Age at 6 April 1997	Earnings £
Under 36	84,000
36-45	96,000
46-50	120,000
51-55	126,000
56-60	130,666
Over 60	122,182

Illustration
Veronica Adams aged 48 earns £140,000 per annum. She has an existing retirement annuity and contributes £12,000 each year.

Veronica's maximum contribution limits are:

(1) Into her retirement annuity – £24,500 (17½% x £140,000)

(2) Into a personal pension – £21,000 (25% x £84,000)

Veronica can either contribute:

(a) A further £12,500 into her retirement annuity, or

(b) A premium into a personal pension plan. If she chooses to do so the total additional contributions she can make into the new personal pension and her existing retirement annuity between them are £9,000.

If your earnings are below the amounts in the above table you should again contribute the maximum amount into your existing retirement annuity and top this up by paying a further premium into a personal pension plan.

Illustration
Alan Potter aged 57 earns £88,000 per annum. He has a retirement annuity and pays premiums of £13,000 annually.

Alan's maximum contribution limits are:

(1) Into his retirement annuity – £19,800 (22½% × £88,000)

(2) Into a personal pension – £29,400 (35% × £84,000)

Alan can either contribute:

(a) A further £6,800 into his retirement annuity and pay a personal pension premium of £9,600, or

(b) An amount of £16,400 into a personal pension.

10

INVESTMENT INCOME

Most of you will at some time or other need to look into the various types of investment on offer. Perhaps you will be looking to find a suitable home for regular savings or to invest a more substantial amount such as an inheritance or a lump sum on retirement. Investment or unearned income is that which does not depend on your active involvement or physical effort in some business or trade. Bank or building society interest, dividends on shares or unit trust holdings, rents, income from a trust and interest on government stocks are all investment income.

Tax-free income
The most widely known investments where the return is free of both Income Tax and Capital Gains Tax are some of those available from the Department of National Savings. They are:

- Fixed Interest and Index-linked Savings Certificates;

- Premium Bond Prizes;

- First £70 of annual interest on a National Savings Bank Ordinary Account.

Also tax-free is interest on your TESSA, provided you do not touch the capital, income from your PEP investments and any dividends you receive on shares you own in Venture Capital Trusts.

Apart from interest on any National Savings Bank account, no details of these need to be shown on your annual Income Tax Return.

Rental income
The letting of property, including isolated or casual lettings, is treated as a business for tax purposes. This applies to a flat, house, shop or any other property which you let out to tenants. Most of the rules currently in force for working out the taxable profits from a trade or profession also apply in calculating your annual profits from let property. All income from property situated in the United Kingdom is pooled together, regardless of the type of lease. It does not matter whether the property is furnished or unfurnished. Losses from your business of renting out property can be carried forward to be set against future profits of your income from property business.

Apart from expenditure of a capital nature, such as that on structural alterations or improvements, the general running costs of a property can be set against rental income. Allowable expenses include:

- costs of letting out the property including estate agents' fees, advertising expenses and the costs of drawing up an inventory;

- interest relating to your property letting business. It matters not whether the interest is payable on a loan or overdraft;

- rent collection costs;

- maintenance, repairs and redecorations;

- premiums on buildings and contents insurance policies;

- rent and water rates;

- Council Tax which you pay for your tenants;

- all other expenses of managing the property such as stationery, postage, etc.;

- your share of expenditure on the common parts of the let property.

Illustration

	£	£
Rent receivable from let property		12,000
Less: Expenses		
Rent collection costs	1,410	
Council Tax	440	
Water rates	120	
Building insurance premium	260	
Roof repairs	752	
Garden maintenance	210	
		3,192
1997/98 net rental income		£8,808

If your gross rental income before expenses is less than £15,000 in the year, you do not need to list the expenses separately. The total expenses can be entered on your Return as one amount.

Where you are renting out property which is unfurnished, you can claim capital allowances on the cost of fixtures, fittings and equipment incurred on the let property.

If you are letting a furnished property you can claim an additional deduction to cover the cost of wear and tear to furnishings and fittings. This can be what you actually spend on renewing fixtures and fittings. Alternatively you can claim a fixed allowance of 10% of the rent less amounts paid out on water rates and Council Tax. If the property in the preceding illustration is let furnished this allowance would be £1,144 as follows:

Illustration

	£
Rent receivable	12,000
Less: Water rates and Council Tax	560
	£11,440
Wear and tear allowance: 10%	£1,144

The rules dealing with the taxation of premiums on leases are more complicated and outside the scope of this book.

Rent-a-Room

Income from the furnished letting of spare rooms in your home is tax-free providing the annual gross rents do not exceed £4,250 per annum. The space you let out must be in your only or main home. This can be a house, flat, caravan or even a houseboat. You can choose to opt out of the special form of relief. You will then be taxed under the normal rules dealing with income from furnished lettings. If, for example, there was a loss on the letting which could be set against other income then it would pay you to make the opt-out election.

Where your annual gross rents are more than £4,250 then you can pay tax on the excess gross rents, without any relief for expenses, or under the rules for taxing furnished lettings income.

Illustration
Theresa Stevens lets a room in her house for £4,800 per annum. The expenses which can be set against the income total £1,400. Under the Rent-a-Room relief her Income Tax liability is £126.50 (£4,800 – £4,250) x 23%. Alternatively, under the normal rules, the tax liability would total £782 (£4,800 – £1,400) x 23%.

It is necessary to make an election if you want to adopt the simple method of paying Income Tax on the gross rents over £4,250 per annum.

Where more than one individual is entitled to income under the Rent-a-Room scheme the £4,250 limit is halved. Each lessor's exempt amount is then £2,125. This rule means that a married couple taking in lodgers should be able to arrange their affairs in such a way that the letting income is divisible between them (each spouse will then have a limit of £2,125); or goes wholly to either husband or wife (in which case either spouse will be due the full £4,250 limit).

Dividends and interest

The tables below set out the types of investment where the dividends and interest are paid to the investor after deduction of Income Tax, together with those where no such deduction is made.

Tax credit of 20%
Dividends on shares
Income distributions on unit trust holdings

Tax deducted at 20%
Building society interest
Interest on British government stocks, with some exceptions
Bank deposit interest
National Savings First Option Bonds
Purchased life annuities – income element

Interest not taxed at source
Interest on certain British Government stocks
National Savings Bank ordinary and investment accounts
National Savings Income and Capital Bonds
National Savings Pensioners' Guaranteed Income Bonds
Certificates of Tax Deposit
Single deposits over £50,000 for a fixed period of not more than 5 years
Deposits with non-UK branches of banks and building societies

As the above tables indicate, the rate at which Income Tax is charged on income from savings – dividends and interest – is at the lower rate of 20%. Furthermore your savings income is treated as the top part of your taxable income so that:

- non-taxpayers will only be able to claim repayment of Income Tax at 20% on their savings income;

- for individuals who are liable to Income Tax at the lower rate the tax of 20% withheld at source will match their exact liability;

- taxpayers who are liable at the basic rate of 23%, but not the top rate, will not face any further tax charge on their savings income;

- individuals who are liable to tax at 40% will be required to pay Income Tax of a further 20% each year to the extent that their savings income takes them above the basic rate band and into the higher rate.

Illustrations

1. Derek Bridge receives savings income, including tax deducted at source, of £600 for 1997/98. His other income, after allowances and reliefs, comes to £4,600. He pays tax for the year as follows:

On the first	£4,100 @ 20%
On the next	£500 @ 23%
On his savings income of	£600 @ 20%

2. Davina Wright banks savings income of £8,000, including tax deducted at source, during 1997/98. From other sources she receives income of £20,000 after allowances and reliefs. Her tax charge is worked out as follows:

On the first	£4,100 @ 20%
On the next	£15,900 @ 23%
On her savings income of	£6,100 @ 20%
On the final	£1,900 @ 40%

The £6,100 slice of savings income attracts tax at the rate of 20% as it falls within the limit of income of £26,100 taxed at the lower and basic rates.

Many people mistakenly assume – because the dividends and interest mentioned in the top two tables are paid after tax has been deducted – that they need not be reported on their annual Tax Return. This misunderstanding is most particularly associated with building society interest. Whatever the amount of your dividends and interest these details must be shown on your Tax Return. The size of this income may be such as to give rise to a liability to tax at the higher rate.

Individuals not liable to tax can arrange to receive their interest gross. This is done by completing special forms which are available at Banks, Building Societies, Post Offices and Tax Offices throughout the country. Individual savers who are not liable to tax, but receive interest from which tax has been deducted, can claim repayment from the Inland Revenue. These measures benefit non-earning married women, pensioners, children and other individuals not liable to Income Tax who choose to invest their savings in Banks and Building Societies.

The current-year basis of taxation now extends to the taxing of investment income received where tax is not deducted at source such as interest on the various National Savings Bonds or accounts listed in the earlier table. For sources commencing after 5 April 1994 the current year rules apply immediately. Where, however, the investment income with no tax deducted at source first arose before 6 April 1994, and continues beyond 5 April 1998, the interest received will be taxed as follows:

Year of Assessment	Basis of Taxation	Interest Taxed
1995/96	Preceding year basis	Interest received in year ended 5 April 1995
1996/97	Transitional year	50% x actual interest in the two years to 5 April 1997
1997/98	Current year basis	Interest credited in the year to 5 April 1998

Accrued income

Interest on fixed-rate investments is treated as accruing on a day-to-day basis between payment dates. On a sale the vendor is charged to Income Tax on the accrued interest from the previous payment date to the date of the transaction. The purchaser is allowed to deduct this amount from the interest which he receives on the following payment date. These arrangements cover both fixed and variable-rate stocks and bonds, including those issued by governments, companies and local authorities. The arrangements will not affect you if the nominal value of your securities is under £5,000.

Illustration

The interest on a holding of 8% Treasury Stock 2000 is payable on each 7 June and 7 December. The half-yearly interest on a holding of £20,000, sold for settlement on 12 August 1997, is £800.

Accrued proportion = $\frac{66}{183}$ x £800 = £288.52

Offshore funds

You may have an investment in an Offshore Fund which distributes substantially all its income by way of dividend. If this is so then the regular dividends you receive are taxed as income and any profit or loss on sale will rank as either a capital gain or loss for the purposes of Capital Gains Tax (see Chapter 13).

Perhaps, however, the Fund pays no dividends and simply accumulates all the income it receives. Then, all the profit on sale is chargeable to Income Tax even if part of the gain could reasonably be considered to represent a capital profit.

Overseas investment income

Generally, income from investments abroad is

- taxed in the same way as the gross interest paid on the various National Savings Investments mentioned earlier on in this chapter;

- now taxed in accordance with the rules governing the new current year basis of taxation;

- considered to be income from savings like any other dividends or interest income.

Non-qualifying life policies

Investment Bonds and Guaranteed Income Bonds offered by most life assurance companies fall within this category. A lump sum premium is paid at the outset. The investor can usually make partial withdrawals from the Bond, draw an income or leave it untouched until it is cashed in or forms part of his estate on death. No tax relief is due on the single premium. The proceeds of a Bond are not liable to Capital Gains Tax or Income Tax at the basic rate. There can be a liability to tax at the higher rate of 40% on chargeable events. These arise on surrender or maturity of the policy, on death of the life assured, or on withdrawals in excess of the cumulative allowance built up at the time.

At the end of each policy year, an allowance of 5% of the original investment is given. This can be carried forward from year to year. It follows that over a period of 20 years allowances of up to 100% of the initial investment will be given. A taxable gain only arises if the amount of a withdrawal is more than the cumulative allowances at the time. It is the excess which is taxed.

Illustration

Edward Clark invests £8,000 in an Investment Bond. Withdrawals of £700 and £2,300 are made during the third and sixth policy years. The annual allowance is £400 being 5% of the original investment. A taxable gain of £600 arises in year six as follows:

Number of Policy Years	Cumulative Allowance	Amount Withdrawn	Cumulative Withdrawls	Taxable Amount
	£	£	£	£
1	400	–	–	–
2	800	–	–	–
3	1,200	700	700	–
4	1,600	–	700	–
5	2,000	–	700	–
6	2,400	2,300	3,000	600

When the final chargeable event on a Bond occurs, the taxable gain is calculated by taking into account all previous withdrawals and taxable gains.

Illustration

The Investment Bond in the illustration above is encashed after 9 years for £9,506. The taxable gain amounts to £3,906 as follows:

	£	£
Policy proceeds		9,506
Add: Withdrawals in years 3 and 6		3,000
		12,506
Less: Original investment	8,000	
Amount already taxed	600	
		8,600
Taxable gain on encashment		**£3,906**

The method of calculating the higher rate Income Tax due on the taxable gain involves a number of stages including *top slicing* relief.

Illustration

Edward Clark, who made a gain of £3,906 on the final encashment of his Investment Bond featured in the two earlier illustrations, is a single man. During 1997/98 his other income, all earnings, amounted to £30,000.

Gain on encashment of Bond	£3,906
Number of years held	9
Taxable slice of gain	£434
Taxable income – excluding slice of gain	£
Earnings	30,000
Less: Personal allowance	4,045
	£25,955

Tax applicable to slice of gain	
On first £145 (£26,100-£25,955) @ 0%	–
On next £289 (excess over £26,100)	
@17% (40%-23%)	£49.13
Average rate on slice	11.32%
The tax payable on the gain =	
£3,906 @ 11.32% =	£442.17

Tax-Exempt Special Savings Accounts

You can invest in a Tax-Exempt Special Savings Account if you are over 18 and resident in the UK. A TESSA is a Savings Scheme with a Bank, Building Society or other institution where the interest is tax free. Each individual is only allowed one TESSA.

Husbands and wives are treated separately so they can each start up their own TESSA. The account must run for a full five years. The freedom from Income Tax on the interest will be lost if any part of the capital is withdrawn during the five year investment period.

As TESSAs are primarily aimed to encourage the small saver the investment limit is relatively modest. Up to £9,000 may be invested over the five year period. In the first year the maximum savings limit is £3,000. This reduces to £1,800 in each subsequent year but the overall limit of £9,000 must not be exceeded. Individuals can use a TESSA to make regular monthly savings or to deposit lump sums as and when they can. For example, both the following savings patterns are within the rules:

Year	Amount Invested	
	£	£
1	3,000	2,200
2	1,800	1,800
3	1,800	None
4	1,800	1,500
5	600	1,800
	£9,000	£7,300

Investors can withdraw interest as it arises during the investment period. Up to the full amount of interest which has been credited to the account can be paid out at any time. However, an amount equivalent to the basic rate of Income Tax on the withdrawal must be retained within the TESSA. The Income Tax left in the account can be withdrawn in full at the end of the five-year period. At that time a TESSA will cease to be a tax-exempt fund and any further interest credited to the account will be taxable in the normal way.

If an investor dies during the period when the account is tax free, it comes to an end but none of the tax benefits up to that time are lost.

When a TESSA matures you can put all the capital – up to £9,000 – into a follow-up TESSA which must be opened within six months of the date the original TESSA matured. It may be held with the same institution or a different one. If you decide to open a follow-up account with a different institution you will be able to get a certificate from the institution which held your first TESSA at maturity. This is evidence of your entitlement to an enhanced first year deposit — up to £9,000 — in your new account with a different bank, Building Society or similar institution.

All the paperwork required by the Inland Revenue will be handled by the institution with which you have your TESSA. You will not need to mention the tax-free interest on your TESSA in your annual Tax Return.

Personal Equity Plans

Personal Equity Plans (PEPs) are a tax-free way of investing in shares. Any dividends you receive on your investments are exempt from Income Tax. There is no Capital Gains Tax to pay on profits made on selling shares within the plan. You do not have to report your dividend income and capital gains to the Inland Revenue on your annual Tax Return.

You can set up a plan so long as you are over 18 and resident in the UK for tax purposes. The maximum amount you can invest each tax year in a PEP is £6,000. Husbands and wives are treated individually so they are both allowed to set up their own plans each year within the maximum investment limit. There are plans which cater for either lump sum investments or regular monthly contributions.

The same plan can invest in:

- ordinary shares of UK companies or comparable shares issued by European Community companies. The UK ordinary shares must be quoted on the UK Stock Exchange or dealt with on the Unlisted Securities Market. The ordinary shares of other EC companies must be officially listed on a recognised stock exchange in the European Community;

- preference shares of UK and European Community companies;

- a range of corporate bonds and convertibles issued by UK non-financial companies. The corporate bonds must have a minimum term of at least five years to maturity and be issued at a fixed rate of interest;

- unit and investment trusts which hold at least 50% of their assets in the above investments.

You can invest up to £1500 of your annual subscription limit in a trust which does not have at least 50% of its own investments in UK or EC companies. Such trusts must, however, hold at least half of their assets in ordinary shares. You can also subscribe for new issue shares such as government privatizations, and transfer them into a PEP. This must be done within 42 days from the time they are allotted to you. There is no limit on the amount of cash that can be held in a plan. All interest is tax free providing the cash is eventually invested in shares or unit trusts.

In addition to the normal investment limit of £6,000 in a general PEP you can put up to £3,000 each tax year in a PEP which, in turn, invests in the shares of a single company. Shares acquired by members of an Approved All Employee Scheme can be transferred direct to a single company PEP, subject, of course, to the £3,000 limit. The transfer must be made within six weeks from the end of the qualifying period to avoid a liability to Capital Gains Tax.

To set up a PEP you will need to use a plan manager. These are individuals or companies specifically authorized to make investments on your behalf and must be approved by the Inland Revenue. You are the owner of the shares, unit trusts or investment trusts but they are held for you by the plan manager who also deals with all other aspects of the administration of your plan, including the claims for tax reliefs and exemptions to the Inland Revenue.

There are no Income Tax or Capital Gains Tax penalties on withdrawing from or closing down a plan.

Friendly Societies
All individuals, including children under 18, can invest up to £270 per annum in a tax-exempt savings plan with a Friendly Society. A family with two children can now save as much as £1,080 per annum through this type of investment.

Enterprise Investment Scheme
The aims of the Scheme are twofold:

- to provide a targeted incentive for equity investment in unquoted trading companies which will help overcome the problems faced by such companies in raising small amounts of equity finance;

- to encourage outside investors, who introduce finance and expertise to a company, by enabling them to take an active part in the management of the company as paid directors without losing entitlement to relief.

The Scheme provides Income Tax relief at 20% on qualifying investments up to £100,000 in any tax year. Investors are allowed either Income Tax or Capital Gains Tax relief for losses made on the disposal of qualifying shares. All shares in a qualifying company must be held for at least five years. Investors previously unconnected with a qualifying company or its trade can become directors whilst still eligible for relief on their investment. Relief on up to one-half of the amount that an individual invests between 6 April and 5 October in any tax year can be carried back to the previous tax year, subject to a maximum limit of £15,000.

Qualifying companies are unquoted trading companies which carry on a qualifying activity for a minimum of three years. They are able to raise up to £1 million a year through the Scheme. The Scheme extends to companies which are trading in the United Kingdom whether or not they are incorporated and resident here. Companies investing in private rented housing are outside the Scheme.

Venture Capital Trusts

The Venture Capital Trust Scheme is aimed at generating equity investment in dynamic, innovative, unquoted trading companies. Individuals who invest in Venture Capital Trusts are eligible for Income Tax incentives. They are entitled to Income Tax relief at 20% on subscriptions up to £100,000 in any tax year for new ordinary shares providing the shares are held for at least five years. Also any dividends declared and paid by Venture Capital Trusts are tax free. Their shares must be quoted on the Stock Exchange.

Joint income

Many married couples have Bank or Building Society accounts, Unit Trust Holdings or other share investments, or property held in their joint names. They are then treated as if they own the account or asset equally and each will have to pay Income Tax on half the annual income. Alternatively, if capital invested in a Building Society account in joint names actually belongs to husband and wife in unequal shares they can be taxed on their respective shares of the income. The married couple must then declare to the Inland Revenue how the account or other property and the income are shared between them. There is a special form to complete. The declaration applies from the date it is made.

Where one spouse transfers an income-producing asset to the other spouse knowing or expecting that the income will be credited to a joint account on which the donor spouse is free to draw, the income will still be regarded as belonging to the donor spouse for tax purposes.

11

THE FAMILY UNIT

Until the system of Independent Taxation was introduced some seven years ago, our tax laws were built round the concept of the family unit. This is no longer so. Now, husbands and wives are taxed separately on their income and capital gains. They must complete their own Tax Returns each year and are each responsible for settling their respective tax liabilities.

Marriage

Husband and wife are each entitled to personal allowances which can be set against their own income each year, whether this be from earnings or from investments. They can each have taxable income, after allowances and reliefs, of £26,100 for 1997/98 before either of them is liable to tax at the higher 40% rate. They may, of course, need to make some re-arrangements to their affairs if they are to take full advantage of opportunities to save tax under Independent Taxation.

Children

A child is treated as a separate individual for tax purposes like anyone else. A wage that your son or daughter receives, for example, for a weekend job in the local newsagent's shop is taxable. However, a child is also entitled to the personal allowance so no tax should actually be payable on the earnings.

If all this tempts you to think about giving some of your savings to your children so that the Income Tax on the interest or dividends can be recovered by being set off against their personal allowances, then I must warn you to proceed with caution. The income from a gift by a parent in favour of an unmarried minor/child is still regarded as the parent's income for tax purposes if it is paid out or applied for the child's benefit. If the income is accumulated, it will be treated as belonging to the child. Neither income nor capital should be used until the child is 18.

One way of using some of a child's personal allowance is by taking full advantage of the tax-free investment income a child can receive on capital from his or her parents. This annual limit is currently £100. This means that a married couple with two children can give away capital which will generate up to £400 in income per annum. Separate accounts should be opened for each child for the gifts from each parent. If, for some reason, the £100 limit is surpassed, the whole income – not just the excess over £100 – becomes taxable. Grandparents or other relatives can, however, give savings to their grandchildren or nieces, nephews, etc., without the same restrictions.

Most parents opt for either a building society or bank deposit account when investing their child's savings. In the previous chapter on investment income (Chapter 10), I mentioned that interest on, for example, a National Savings Bank investment account is not taxed at source, unlike that on a bank or building society account where the interest is paid to the investor after deduction of tax at the basic rate. Savers who are not taxpayers can receive gross interest on their bank or building society investments. This will be of considerable benefit to children. I also referred to these arrangements in more detail in the previous chapter.

As an alternative to a bank or building society account for your child's savings, why not take a look at the Children's Bonus Bonds issued by the Department for National Savings. They are particularly suitable for gifts from parents. The return on these bonds is exempt from both Income Tax and Capital Gains Tax. This tax exemption means that no parent can be liable to Income Tax on interest arising on the gift.

There is no general tax allowance for children. However, you will probably be able to claim the additional personal allowance if you are single and have a child living with you (Chapter 3).

Responsibility for completing a minor's Income Tax Repayment Claim rests with the child's trustee or guardian. A minor child is also a taxable person for the purposes of Capital Gains Tax (Chapter 13) and Inheritance Tax (Chapter 17).

Separation and divorce

Not only can the breakdown of a marriage cause much personal suffering, particularly when there are children of the marriage, but invariably it also calls for a reorganization of the parted couple's financial affairs. The full married couple's allowance is due in the year of separation.

I referred in Chapter 3 to the additional personal allowance and the situations when it can be claimed. When a couple split up any children of the marriage usually go and live with their mother. She can claim the additional personal allowance. Nevertheless, where a couple have at least two children it may be possible for both their father and mother to benefit from the additional personal allowance. Each would claim for one of the children.

Special rules apply to the tax treatment of maintenance payments under arrangements made before 15 March 1988. These rules extend to Court Orders which had been applied for by that date and were actually made before the end of June of that year. All maintenance payments under Separation Agreements or Court Orders must be made without deduction of tax at the basic rate. The tax relief allowed to the payer is the lower of:

- the maintenance paid in the tax year; and

- the maintenance paid in the year to 5 April 1989.

Tax relief on the first £1,830 of payments is restricted to 15%. The excess is deductible from the payer's income in calculating the amount of tax he or she pays.

The recipient of maintenance is taxed on the same amount on which the payer gets tax relief, less a deduction equivalent to the married couple's allowance for the year.

Illustration

Under a Court Order made in 1986 Ian Watkins has to pay his ex-wife, June, maintenance of £8,000. When the Court Order was made the annual amount payable was only £5,000. It was increased by £3,000 in 1990. Another Court Order was made in 1991. The annual maintenance under this second Order is £2,000. In 1997/98 Ian's income totalled £35,000, comprising earnings of £33,000 and bank interest before tax of £2,000. The calculation of the tax payable by Ian of £6,279.50 for 1997/98 is:

	£	£
Earnings		33,000
Bank interest		2,000
		35,000
Less:		
Personal allowance	4,045	
Deductible maintenance (£5,000 less £1,830)	3,170	
		7,215
Taxable income		£27,785
Income Tax payable:		
£4,100 @ 20%		820.00
£22,000 @ 23%		5,060.00
£1,685 @ 40%		674.00
		6,554.00
Less: Relief for maintenance payments –		
£1,830 @ 15%		274.50
		£6,279.50

Tax relief for the payments under the 1986 Court Order is restricted to the amount of £5,000 paid in 1988/89. No tax relief can be given for the payments under the 1991 Order as at least £1,830 is being claimed for the 1986 Order.

As an alternative you can elect to switch over to the new rules. These apply to Court Orders and maintenance agreements made on or after 15 March 1988. The divorced or separated spouse will only qualify for tax relief on payments where these are made to the other party to the marriage. The maintenance can be for the former or separated spouse or in respect of any child of the family. The maximum amount on which tax relief is given in any tax year is the difference between the married and single allowances; currently this is £1,830, on which the tax relief is limited to 15%. No tax must be deducted at source from such payments. They are tax free in the hands of the recipient.

The Child Support Agency has taken over much of the work of the Courts on child maintenance. Maintenance assessed by the Agency qualifies for tax relief in the same way as maintenance under a court order. Furthermore, maintenance collected by the Agency on behalf of the divorced or separated spouse of the pair qualifies for tax relief in the same way as if the maintenance had been paid direct to the spouse.

Old age

Unfortunately, the elderly taxpayer has to cope with the tax system in exactly the same way as everyone else. Nevertheless, there are some factors which are only relevant in calculating the tax payable on the elderly person's income. First and foremost are the age allowances. In Chapter 3 I explained how a pensioner calculates whether he or she is entitled to these allowances.

Pensions, apart from the war disablement and widow's pensions, are taxable. These include a pension from either the State, a retirement annuity, a personal pension or a past employer's fund. The State Pension includes:

- The basic retirement (or old person's) pension;

- A state earnings-related pension (SERPS);

- A graduated pension;

- The age addition if you are over 80.

Although it is taxable, no tax is deducted at source from the State Pension. In addition to including a pensioner's personal allowances in the coding notice of a pension taxed under PAYE it will also incorporate a deduction equivalent to the State Retirement Pension. In this way the tax due on it is collected. The need to make a direct tax payment is avoided.

A code number ending with 'V' indicates a pensioner is entitled to the married couple's age allowance for age 65-74. A coding which includes the personal age allowance for 65-74 finishes up with 'P'. If you are entitled to the higher age allowances for age 75 or over, your coding will end with the letter 'T'. The same applies where you do not receive the full age allowances because your income is over £15,600. In the exceptional situation of the deduction for the State Retirement Pension exceeding a pensioner's personal allowances, the Inland Revenue now issue a 'K' coding. The amount of the negative allowance is then added to your pension on which tax is to be paid.

When a person starts to draw the old age pension, the Department of Social Security sends out a form to find out the tax office which deals with the pensioner's Tax Return. This enables the Department to tell the tax office of the amount of a new pensioner's State Pension and subsequent increases. This makes sure the correct deduction for the State Pension is always included in a pensioner's code number.

With careful planning an elderly married couple with modest incomes may well be able to generate significant savings in their tax bills as the following example demonstrates.

Illustration

Gordon and Hilda Kelly, an elderly married couple, both in their late 60s, whose joint income for 1997/98 amounted to £26,000, paid Income Tax of £3,179.15 for the year. This all related to Gordon's income as follows:

	Gordon £	Hilda £
State Pensions	3,247	1,942
Occupational Pensions	7,653	1,058
Building Society Interest		
– Gross equivalent	7,000	–
Interest on British Government Stocks	3,000	2,100
	20,900	5,100
Less: Personal Allowance	4,045	5,220
Taxable Income	£16,855	£–
Income Tax Payable		
£4,100 @ 20%	820.00	–
£2,755 @ 23%	633.65	–
£10,000 @ 20% (savings income)	2,000.00	–
	3,453.65	–
Less: Relief for married couple's allowance – £1,830 @ 15%	274.50	–
	£3,179.15	£–

Gordon's income is above the upper limit beyond which he is not due either the personal age or married couple's age allowances. Also Hilda has insufficient income to benefit from her full personal age allowance.

Significant tax savings of £497.50 for 1997/98 could have been achieved by the couple if Gordon had transferred capital to Hilda as follows:

	Gordon	Hilda
	£	£
State Pensions	3,247	1,942
Occupational Pensions	7,653	1,058
Building Society Interest		
– Gross equivalent	3,500	3,500
Interest on British Government Stocks	1,000	4,100
	15,400	10,600
Less: Personal Allowance	5,220	5,220
Taxable Income	£10,180	£5,380

Income Tax Payable		
£4,100 @ 20%	820.00	820.00
£1,580/– @ 23%	363.40	–
£4,500/£1,280 @ 20% (savings income)	900.00	256.00
	2,083.40	1,076.00
Less: Relief for married couple's age allowance – £3,185 @ 15%	477.75	–
	£1,605.65	£1,076.00

Death

Sadly, death comes to all of us and has consequences for taxation. There is no reduction in either the married couple's or married couple's age allowance, as the case may be, in the year of death of either spouse.

If the husband dies first he is entitled to his full personal allowance in the year of death. If his income that year is such that he is unable to use up the full married couple's or married couple's age allowance then the balance can be transferred to his widow. A widow can claim the widow's bereavement allowance for both the tax year in which her husband dies and the following tax year as long as she has not remarried by the beginning of that year.

Where the wife dies before her husband she will be due the full personal or, if appropriate, personal age allowance in the year of death.

12

THE OVERSEAS ELEMENT

Apart from some special cases, the amount of tax you pay each year depends on whether you are resident in the United Kingdom (UK) and, to a lesser extent, on your domicile status. If you live permanently in the UK then, generally, all your income arising in this country will be liable to UK taxation. Overseas income is similarly taxable although special rules apply in taxing foreign income of individuals not domiciled in the UK.

Not only are the two concepts of domicile and residence of fundamental importance in determining the extent of an individual's liability to UK taxation on income, they are of equal significance for the purposes of both Capital Gains Tax and Inheritance Tax.

Domicile

Your domicile will generally be considered to be the country or state which you regard as your permanent homeland. Your domicile is separate from your residence or nationality. When you are born you acquire a domicile of origin from your father. You can abandon your original domicile by birth if you settle in another country or state with a view to making it your new permanent home. Providing you sever all links with your current country of domicile you can move towards acquiring a domicile of choice in the new country. You should be prepared to provide a substantial amount of evidence that you propose to live there for ever.

A wife's domicile is not necessarily the same as her husband's domicile if they were married at some time after the end of 1973. It is decided by the same factors as for any other individual who is able to have an independent domicile. A woman who married before the beginning of 1974 automatically acquired the domicile of her husband on marriage. So long as the marriage lasts, her domicile only alters when there is any change in the domicile of her husband.

If you think you have good grounds for believing that you should not be regarded as domiciled in the UK you should write to your tax office about this. Usually, you can then expect to receive a questionnaire which you should fill in and send back to your tax office. The information you have supplied will be considered by the Inland Revenue Specialist Department which deals with these matters. In due course you will receive a ruling on your domicile status.

Residence and ordinary residence

There is no statutory definition of residence and ordinary residence. Each case must be judged on the facts. What follows is a summary of the main factors which will be taken into account.

Without exception you will always be regarded as resident in the UK if you spend 183 days or more here in the tax year. Days of arrival in, and departure from, the UK are normally left out of account in working out the number of days spent here.

If you are here for less than 183 days you will still be treated as resident where you visit the UK regularly and after four tax years your visits during those years average 91 days or more in a tax year. From the fifth year you are treated as UK resident.

You are also regarded as ordinarily resident in the UK if you are resident here from year to year. It is possible to be resident, but not ordinarily resident. For example, you may normally live outside the UK but are in this country for at least 183 days in a tax year. Conversely you can occasionally be considered to be ordinarily resident, not but actually resident, for a particular tax year. This could happen if you live in the UK but, for some reason, are abroad for a complete tax year.

Working abroad – long absences

Poor job prospects in the UK, together with higher salaries and low taxation abroad, may prompt you to look for work overseas. This is likely to involve living abroad permanently for a time. Your probable residence status is clearly set out in paragraphs 2:2 and 2:3 of the Inland Revenue booklet IR20 – *Residents and Non-Residents* – as follows:

If you leave the UK to work full time abroad under a contract of employment, you are treated as not resident and not ordinarily resident if you meet all the following conditions:

- your absence from the UK and your employment abroad both last for at least a whole tax year;

- during your absence any visits you make to the UK

  – total less than 183 days in any tax year, and

  – average less than 91 days a tax year (the average is taken over the period of absence up to a maximum of four years; any dates spent in the UK because of exceptional circumstances beyond your control, for example the illness of yourself or a member of your immediate family, are not normally counted for this purpose).

If you meet all of the above conditions you are treated as not resident and not ordinarily resident in the UK from the day after you leave the UK to the date before you return to the UK at the end of your employ-ment abroad. You are treated as coming to the UK permanently on the day you return from your employment abroad and as resident and ordinarily resident from that date.

There will be no tax to pay here on your salary for the part of the tax year after you have left the UK.

There is no specific definition of when employment abroad is 'full time'. Each particular case must be considered on all the facts. Nevertheless, where your employment involves a standard pattern of hours, it will be regarded as full time if your working hours each week are comparable with those that would be worked in the UK. Furthermore, several part time jobs all at the same time could be taken as constituting full time employment.

If you leave the UK to work full-time in a trade, profession or vocation overseas and fulfil the same conditions as anyone taking up full-time employment abroad then your UK residence status will be determined in the same way.

You may well take your spouse with you. By concession he or she may also be regarded as neither resident nor ordinarily resident for the same period even if your spouse does not work abroad.

Working abroad – shorter absences

Where your job takes you overseas for shorter periods of absence then your tax treatment in the UK is still worked out on a favourable basis. Providing you can establish a consecutive period of at least 365 days working overseas, the exemption from Income Tax on the earnings from that employment is 100%. You are allowed intermittent visits to the UK in establishing a qualifying period of at least 365 days. These must not amount to more than 62 days, nor in building up the qualifying period must they come to more than one-sixth of the period starting from the outset.

Illustration

Cynthia Bishop, a businesswoman, leaves the UK and is away for 102 days. She returns for 15 days before leaving for a further spell of 80 days. She then holidays in the UK for 14 days before a final period abroad of 160 days. All the periods can be linked up to make one qualifying period of 371 days.

Working abroad – expenses

Tax relief is allowed on travel expenses you incur in relation to your overseas employment. Nor will you be taxed on the cost of board and lodging provided for you where the expenses are borne by your employer.

Generally, whenever your job takes you overseas, even for short periods, you will not be taxed on the cost of your travelling expenses so long as your employer meets the bills. This also applies to the costs of unlimited return visits to the UK during longer assignments abroad.

No taxable benefit arises where your employer meets the travelling costs of your spouse and children to visit you overseas. Not more than two return visits by the same person are allowed each year, and you must be working abroad for a continuous period of at least 60 days.

Leaving the UK permanently

Where you go abroad to live permanently, or to live outside the UK for three years or more, you will provisionally be considered neither resident nor ordinarily resident in the UK from the day following your departure. You should be prepared to provide sufficient evidence of your intention to make a permanent home somewhere outside the UK. Providing you do not infringe the rules about visits to the UK the provisional non-resident ruling will subsequently be confirmed by the Inland Revenue. You are entitled to full allowances and reliefs for the year of departure.

Before you leave, ask your Tax Office for the special form (P85) to be completed by individuals going abroad. The information in the form about your intended residence position will enable the Inland Revenue to make an in-year tax refund to you if, for example, you are claiming split-year treatment.

When you become not ordinarily resident in the UK you can apply to receive interest on any bank or building society account here without deduction of tax. Similarly, Income Tax is not charged on the interest from certain UK Government Securities.

Calculating annual average visits

The set formula to be used in working out the average number of days spent in the UK each year is:

$$\frac{\text{total visits to the UK (in days)}}{\text{total period since leaving (in days)}} \times 365 \text{ days} = \text{annual average visits}$$

The maximum period over which the average is taken is 4 years.

Illustration

Thomas Winter, a retired solicitor, left the UK on 23 November 1995.
In the period from the date of his departure to 5 April 1996 he visited
the UK for 43 days. In the following three tax years he spent 110, 85 and
57 days in the UK. The average number of days in the UK works out at
87.61 as follows:

$$\frac{43 + 110 + 85 + 57}{133 + 366 + 365 + 365} = \frac{295}{1,229} \times 365 = 87.61 \text{ days}$$

As this is less than the 91 days per annum average Thomas will be
treated as non-resident throughout the period.

Allowances for non-UK residents

You may be able to claim UK tax allowances if you are not resident here.
If you are eligible to claim you will generally be entitled to the same
allowances as an individual resident in the UK. The following individuals
can claim:

- a citizen of the Commonwealth;

- a citizen of a state within the European Economic Area;

- a present or former employee of the British Crown;

- a resident of the Isle of Man or the Channel Islands;

- certain other specific classes of individuals.

Income from UK property

Many individuals choose to rent out their homes while they are away,
particularly when they go to work abroad. You can apply to the Inland
Revenue for a certificate authorizing your tenant, or managing agent,
to make payments of rent to you without deducting UK tax. If no such
certificate is issued, tax at the basic rate must be withheld from all
remittances of rent to you.

Even though you are not resident in the UK you could still be liable
to UK tax on income arising from the letting out of UK property.
This is so, whether or not tax is deducted by your tenant or letting agent.
However you will not actually have any UK tax to pay if your total
income, including your income from property after allowable expenses,
chargeable to UK tax is less than any allowances which you may be
entitled to claim.

Double taxation relief

If you move to a country with which the UK has concluded a Double Tax

Agreement, you may be able to claim partial or full exemption from UK tax on certain types of income from UK sources. Normally, you should be entitled to some measure of relief from UK tax on pensions and annuities, royalties and dividends. Many Double Taxation Agreements contain clauses dealing with the special circumstances of teachers and researchers, students and apprentices, and entertainers and sportsmen/women.

Taking up UK residence

Perhaps you have been working overseas, your contract has come to an end and you are thinking about returning here. Before you take up UK residence again there are some specific tax-planning points which must be considered. For example, any bank deposit or building society accounts should be closed before you return as you could otherwise face the prospect of a charge to UK Income Tax on interest accrued, but not credited, during your period of non-residence.

If the UK is not your normal homeland you should initially be able to satisfy our Inland Revenue Authorities that you have an overseas domicile. Any income from investments here is taxable as it arises. Your overseas investment income is not taxed unless it is actually remitted or enjoyed here. Where your job is with either a UK or an overseas employer, and the duties of your employment are performed wholly in the UK, the full amount of your salary is taxable here. Table 9 at the end of the book is a summary of the scope of liability to Income Tax of earnings.

You will be treated as resident and ordinarily resident from the date you arrive if you are either coming here permanently or intending to stay for at least three years. You will be able to claim full UK personal allowances for the year of arrival.

The Inland Revenue have introduced a number of administrative changes to the way the tax affairs of those coming to the UK for secondments or temporary employments are handled. The changes are designed to enable the residence status and domicile of this particular group of individuals to be dealt with more quickly.

The form which is used to obtain information to decide the residence status (P86), has been revised and simplified. It now includes a section on domicile so that it will be possible, in straightforward cases, to deal with an individual's residence status and domicile together. This will apply, for example, to an individual who has never been domiciled within the UK, has come here only to work and intends to leave the UK once the employment ceases. In less straightforward cases where domicile affects liability to UK taxation, a new form is to be introduced to obtain the further information necessary to determine the individual's domicile.

13

CAPITAL GAINS TAX

As its name implies, Capital Gains Tax is a tax on profits you realize from the disposal of capital assets. As with most other forms of taxation there is the usual list of exceptions to this general rule. Gambling, pools or lottery winnings and personal or professional damages are not taxable. Neither are gains realized on disposing of any of the assets in the following table:

- private cars

- National Savings

- your private residence

- chattels, with an expected life of more than 50 years, sold for less than £6,000

- British government securities and many corporate bonds

- shares issued under the Business Expansion Scheme after 18 March 1986 on their first disposal. For the exemption to apply, the Income Tax relief granted must not have been withdrawn

- shares issued under the Enterprise Investment Scheme on their first disposal, so long as the tax relief has not been withdrawn

- shares in Venture Capital Trusts

- investments in a Personal Equity Plan

- life assurance policies – unless purchased by you

- charitable gifts

- gifts for the public benefit

- foreign currency for personal expenditure.

The list of taxable gains includes profits made from disposing of property, shareholdings, unit trust holdings, works of art and foreign currency for other than personal expenditure.

Rate of tax

For the 1997/98 tax year the first £6,500 of chargeable gains you realize are tax free. Husband and wife are each entitled to the annual exemption limit. Gains in excess of the annual tax-free allowance are charged at your Income Tax rates found by adding the gains to your taxable income.

Illustration

Isaac Woolf realized gains of £14,500 during 1997/98. His taxable income, after personal allowances and reliefs, was £19,000. The Capital Gains Tax he owes for the year is £1,993 as follows:

	£
Realized gains	14,500
Less: Exemption limit	6,500
	£8,000
Tax payable:	
£7,100 @ 23%	1,633
£900 @ 40%	360
1997/98 Capital Gains Tax payable	£1,993

The amount of Capital Gains Tax at 23% is worked out on the difference between the £26,100 limit of income taxable at the lower and basic rates and Isaac's income of £19,000.

Any allowances or reliefs which you are unable to use because your income is too low cannot be set against your capital gains.

Husband and wife

Under Independent Taxation husband and wife are taxed separately on the chargeable gains they realize in a tax year above the annual exemption limit. A married couple living together can transfer assets between them free of tax. The indexation allowance is due up to the date of the transfer. The calculation of the indexation allowance for the transferee on the eventual disposal of the asset is more complicated. This exemption from tax ceases to apply when a couple permanently separate.

In cases where a married couple hold an asset in their joint names, any gain is apportioned between them in the ratio of their respective interests in the asset at the time of disposal. This treatment may not necessarily follow the split of the income for income tax purposes. Here the law generally assumes a married couple are equally entitled to the income even if in fact, this is not so. Where a couple have jointly made a declaration to the Inland Revenue of the ratio in which an asset and the income derived from it are shared between them, the same split will be followed for Capital Gains Tax purposes.

Losses

Losses can be set against gains made in the same tax year. Unused losses can be carried forward to be set against gains in subsequent tax years without time limit. They then reduce the amount of your gains in excess of the annual exemption limit.

Illustration

Sally Rogers had capital losses of £4,100 available for carry-forward at 5 April 1997. During 1997/98 she realized gains of £8,800 and made losses of £900.

Her capital gains position for the year is:

	£	£
Gains realized in the year		8,800
Less: Losses: in the year	900	
brought forward (part)	1,400	
	———	2,300
1997/98 Exemption limit		£6,500

The unused losses of £2,700 can be carried forward to be set against gains in later years.

Losses realized by one spouse cannot be set against gains realized by the other spouse. This restriction on the set-off of losses also extends to unused losses at 5 April 1990. This was the last date before the introduction of Independent Taxation.

A loss arising on the sale or gift of an investment to a person connected with the individual making the disposal can only be set off against a gain from a similar disposal at a later date.

Where the value of an asset becomes negligible or nil, the loss can be claimed without actually disposing of the asset. In these hard-pressed times, and with ever increasing numbers of company failures, this form of loss relief should not be overlooked. The loss arises on the date that the relief is claimed. In practice, however, a two-year period is allowed from the end of the tax year in which the asset became of negligible value.

Another form of loss relief applies if you have subscribed for shares in a trading company not quoted on a recognized Stock Exchange. Where you make a loss on disposing of such shares, or they become worthless, the loss can be set against your income rather than against other capital gains.

The computation of gains

The taxable gain on the disposal of an asset is calculated by making various deductions from the price realized on sale, as follows:

- the cost of acquisition, and

- the incidental costs of buying and selling the asset, and

- any additional expenditure incurred on enhancing the value of the asset during the period of ownership, and

- the indexation allowance.

There are occasions when a different figure from the actual disposal proceeds is substituted in the calculation. For example, this happens when you make a gift or sell an asset at a nominal value to a close member of your family. You must then bring into the computation of the capital gain the open-market value of the asset at the time of disposal.

The date of sale of an asset is taken as the date when the contract for sale is made. The same rule applies to the date of acquisition.

Later on in this chapter I shall deal with the special rules in cases where you dispose of assets you owned on either 6 April 1965 or 31 March 1982.

The indexation allowance

This allowance measures the impact of inflation on both the cost of an asset and any other expenditure you have incurred on enhancing its value. The rules dealing with the calculation of the allowance are:

- the allowance is governed by the movement in the Retail Prices Index in the period of ownership. For assets which you have owned since before April 1982 the starting date for calculating the indexation allowance is March 1982;

- when you dispose of an asset which you acquired before 6 April 1982 the indexation allowance can be calculated on either the market value of the asset at 31 March 1982 or its actual cost, whichever is greater. Where you elect for the capital gains on all disposals of assets which you owned on 31 March 1982 to be worked out on their values at that date, ignoring original costs, the indexation allowance can only be calculated on those values;

- the allowance will not be given where an asset is sold at a loss. Neither can the indexation allowance turn a gain into a loss. It can only serve to reduce a gain to nil.

Table 10 at the end of the book sets out the indexation allowance for assets disposed of between April and December 1997.

Illustration

A freehold property was purchased in November 1987 for £40,000. The legal fees and stamp duty on the purchase came to £1,340. An extension was added in February 1990 at a cost of £9,400.

Contracts for sale were exchanged in July 1997. It was sold for £96,000. The estate agents' commission, including the costs of advertising, and solicitors' fees came to £2,820.

The indexation allowance between November 1987 and July 1997 is 0.523, and from February 1990 to July 1997 is 0.310.

The chargeable gain is £17,906 as follows:

		£	£
Sale price			96,000
Less: Costs of sale			2,820
			93,180
Less:	Acquisition price	40,000	
	Costs of purchase	1,340	
	Enhancement expenditure		
	– extension	9,400	
		50,740	
	Indexation allowance:		
	£41,340 x 0.523	21,620	
	£9,400 x 0.310	2,914	
			75,274
	Chargeable gain		£17,906

Assets owned on 31 March 1982

Gains and losses on disposals of assets which you owned on 31 March 1982 can be calculated solely by reference to their market value at that date, ignoring original costs. In most cases, these rules will mean your capital gains are reduced compared with the calculation based on historical cost only.

Illustration

A freehold property purchased in 1976 for £20,000 was sold in May 1997 for £84,000. At 31 March 1982 it was valued at £39,000. The indexation allowance between March 1982 and May 1997 is 0.975.

The chargeable gain is £6,975 as follows:

	On 31 March 1982 Value		On Historical Cost	
	£	£	£	£
Sale price		84,000		84,000
Less: March 1982 value	39,000		–	
Acquisition cost	–		20,000	
Indexation allowance				
£39,000 x 0.975	38,025		38,025	
		77,025		58,025
		£6,975		£25,975
1997/98 Chargeable gain			£6,975	

Needless to say, there are special rules where the calculations based firstly on the March 1982 value and secondly on historical cost give different results, as follows:

On March 1982 Value	On Historical Cost	Chargeable Gain/Loss
Gain of £3,810	Gain of £2,150	£2,150 Gain
Loss of £515	Loss of £95	£95 Loss
Loss of £490	Gain of £760	neither gain nor loss
Gain of £2,435	Loss of £1,640	neither gain nor loss

You can, however, elect for the capital gains on all disposals of assets which you owned on 31 March 1982 to be worked out by reference to their values at that date, ignoring original costs. Once made, the election cannot be revoked.

Quoted stocks and shares

Prior to 6 April 1982 each shareholding was regarded as a single asset. This was commonly known as a 'pool'. Each additional purchase of the same class of shares or a sale of part of the holding represented either an addition to, or a disposal out of, the pool. With the introduction of the indexation allowance this changed. Each shareholding acquired after 5 April 1982 represented a separate asset. A subsequent addition to a holding you owned at 5 April 1982 could not be added to the pool.

As from 6 April 1985 the rules were altered once more. Shares of the same class are again regarded as a single asset growing or diminishing on each acquisition or disposal. This form of 'pooling' applies to shares acquired after 5 April 1982 unless they had already been disposed of before 6 April 1985; it is called a 'new holding'. A pool which was frozen under the 1982 rules stays that way. It remains a single asset which cannot grow by subsequent acquisitions and is known as a '1982 holding'. The rules are even more complicated where you may still own any shares which were acquired before 6 April 1965.

A '1982 holding' is treated like any other asset in calculating the indexation allowance. This is not so for a 'new holding'. It is to be kept continually indexed each time there is either an addition to or a disposal out of the pool.

The procedure for matching shares sold with their corresponding acquisition is as follows:

- shares acquired on the same day;

- shares acquired in the nine days preceding a disposal on a first-in first-out basis;

- shares comprised in a 'new holding';

- shares within a '1982 holding'.

Illustration

Gareth Davies made the following purchases in the shares of a quoted company:

Date	Number of Shares	Cost
May 1974	1,500	£1,875
Jan 1981	2,500	£3,500
Mar 1985	3,000	£3,900
Feb 1988	2,000	£3,500

In June 1997 he sold 8,000 shares for £25,600. The shares were valued at £1.50 each on 31 March 1982. The indexation allowance is:

0.983 between March 1982 and June 1997
0.117 between March 1985 and February 1988
0.519 between February 1988 and June 1997

5,000 shares sold must first of all be identified with those in the 'new holding' as follows:

	£
Cost of 3,000 shares in March 1985	3,900
Indexation allowance to February 1988 – 0.117	456
	4,356
Cost of 2,000 shares in February 1988	3,500
	7,856
Indexation allowance to June 1997 – 0.519	4,077
	11,933
Proceeds of sale of 5,000 shares	16,000
Chargeable gain	£4,067

The remaining 3,000 shares sold are then identified with part of the shares acquired before 31 March 1982. As the average cost is £1.34 per share it is beneficial to base the capital gain on the share price at 31 March 1982 as follows:

	£
Value of 3,000 shares at March 1982	4,500
Indexation allowance to June 1997 – 0.983	4,423
	8,923
Proceeds of sale of 3,000 shares	9,600
Chargeable gain	£677

The total chargeable gain on the sale is £4,744.

Whenever you receive a bonus issue of shares of the same class as an existing holding the date of their acquisition is the same as that of the original holding.

If you take up a rights issue to subscribe for additional shares in a company where you are already a shareholder, the indexation allowance on the cost price of the extra shares runs from the date they are acquired, not from the date when the original holding was bought.

Where a company in which you have a holding is taken over, and instead of receiving cash you exchange your shares for shares in the new company, no disposal takes place at that time. Your new holding is regarded as having been acquired at the same time and for the same price as the old one. If you receive a mixture of cash and shares in the new company a gain or loss arises on the cash element of the takeover. It is then necessary to apportion the cost price of the old shares, including the indexation allowance up to the date of the take-over, between the cash received and the value of the shareholding in the new company at the time.

One of the consequences of the procedure for matching shares is that the well-known practice of establishing losses by 'bed-and-breakfasting' shares is possible under the simple procedure of sale and repurchase on consecutive days within the same Stock Exchange account.

Unquoted investments
Many of the rules dealing with quoted stocks and shares also apply to computations on disposals of unquoted investments. For example, the indexing rules apply in the same way as they do to quoted shares.

Most of the special rules dealing with unquoted investments apply to assets held at 6 April 1965 when Capital Gains Tax was introduced.

Assets held on 6 April 1965
Following the introduction of rules dealing with assets owned on 31 March 1982, the special rules for assets held on 6 April 1965 are likely to be of less significance. The method of computation is known as 'time-apportionment'. It does not apply to quoted stocks and shares, only to unquoted investments and other assets such as land. Time-apportionment is designed to eliminate from the charge to tax the profit on sale attributable to the period up to 5 April 1965. This result is achieved by assuming that the asset increased in value at a standard rate throughout the period of ownership. It is the gain, net of indexation, that is time-apportioned. For assets other than quoted stocks and shares, acquired before 6 April 1945, the time-apportionment benefit is limited to 20 years.

Instead of relying on the time-apportionment method, a taxpayer can make an irrevocable election for the value of the asset on 6 April 1965 to be substituted in a calculation of the capital gain arising on sale.

Illustration

A property purchased in June 1959 for £5,000 was sold in late April 1997 for £45,000. An election for the 6 April 1965 value is not beneficial. At 31 March 1982 it was worth £20,000. The indexation allowance between March 1982 and April 1997 is 0.967.

The first calculation of the chargeable gain is:

	£
Sale proceeds	45,000
Less: Purchase price	5,000
Gross gain	£40,000

Time-apportionment:

$$\frac{\text{April 1965 to April 1997} \ = \ 384 \text{ months}}{\text{June 1959 to April 1997} \ = \ 454 \text{ months}} \times £40,000 \ = \ £33,832$$

	£
Less: Indexation allowance £20,000 × 0.967	19,340
Chargeable gain	£14,492

The second calculation of the chargeable gain is:

	£	£
Sale proceeds		45,000
Less: 31 March 1982 value	20,000	
Indexation allowance £20,000 × 0.967	19,340	
		39,340
Chargeable gain		£5,660

It is advantageous for the 31 March 1982 value to be used in calculating the capital gain.

A taxpayer can elect for the capital gains or losses on disposals of quoted shares and securities held at 6 April 1965 to be calculated by substituting the 6 April 1965 values for the original costs in all cases. Separate elections must be made for the taxpayer and spouse and they are required both for ordinary shares and for fixed-interest securities. The election for each category is irrevocable. It has to be made within two years of the end of the tax year in which the first sale after 19 March 1968 occurs. If no election is made the capital gain is worked out by comparing the disposal proceeds with the original cost and value of the holding on 6 April 1965.

Where, as is more likely, a taxpayer has elected for the capital gains on disposals of all assets owned on 31 March 1982 to be worked out solely by reference to their values at that date, the above rules setting out the alternatives available for assets held on 6 April 1965 will be superseded.

Valuations

If you need to use any valuations to work out the gain or loss on a disposal, there is a free service from the Inland Revenue to help you to complete your Self-Assessment Tax Return. You may ask your Tax Office to check valutions after you have made the disposal but before you make your Return. Ask for one copy of form CG34 for each valuation you want checked. Then send back the completed form to your Tax Office together with all the other information and documents requested on the form.

If your valuations are agreed they will not subsequently be challenged when you submit your Tax Return unless there are important facts affecting the valuations that you did not mention. If your figures are not agreed the Inland Revenue will put forward alternative valuations.

Your private residence

The profit on a sale of your home is exempt from tax. The exemption extends to the house and its garden or grounds up to half a hectare, including the land on which the house is built. A larger area can qualify for exemption where it can be shown that it was needed to enjoy the house.

Where a home has not been occupied as your private residence throughout the full period of ownership, or, if later, since 31 March 1982, a proportion of the gain on sale becomes taxable. Nevertheless, certain periods of absence are disregarded in determining whether the gain is totally exempt from tax. These are the last three years of ownership in any event and generally those when you have to live away from home because of your work.

Illustration

Ben White realized a capital gain of £68,000 when he sold his home in December 1997. It had been acquired back in May 1988. He was employed abroad between October 1988 and February 1990. In March 1994 he moved out into his new home.

Both the time spent working overseas and the last three years are regarded as periods when the home was the taxpayer's main residence. The chargeable period is, therefore, only nine months and the chargeable gain is £5,321 as follows:

$$\frac{\text{Chargeable period}}{\text{Period of ownership}} = \frac{9 \text{ months}}{15 \text{ months}} \times \text{£68,000} = \text{£5,321}$$

Where part of your home is used exclusively for business purposes the proportion of the profit on sale attributable to the business use is a chargeable gain. Whether part of your home is actually used exclusively for business use is entirely a matter of fact.

If you let part of your home as residential accommodation, the gain on the part which has been let is either wholly or partly exempt from tax. The proportion of the profit on sale which is exempt is the lower of either £40,000 or an amount equivalent to the gain on the part you have occupied as your home. The same applies when you let out your entire home.

Illustration

Bill Gray made a capital gain of £94,000 when he disposed of his home in November 1997. It had been bought in June 1991. Bill and his family lived there until October 1991 and from October 1994 up to the date of sale. In the intervening period it was let. This period of absence was not one when the home was still regarded as Bill's main residence.

The chargeable gain is only £3,949 as follows:

	£	£
Capital gain (period of ownership – 77 months)		94,000
Less: Main residence exemption – 41 months	50,051	
Letting exemption – 36 months (lower of £40,000 or £50,051)	40,000	
	———	90,051
Chargeable gain		£3,949

Alternatively, if you take in lodgers who mix in and eat with your family, the Inland Revenue take the view that no part of the exemption on a sale of your home is lost. Nor should any capital gain arise if you take advantage of the Rent-a-Room scheme mentioned in Chapter 10.

A second home

If you have two homes such as a house or flat in town for use during the weekdays and a cottage in the country for weekends, the profit on sale of only one of them is exempt from tax. Which one counts as your main residence is a matter of fact. It is, however, possible for you to determine this by writing to your tax office. In the election you should request which of your homes you want regarded as your principal private residence for Capital Gains Tax purposes. The election should apply from the date when you first have at least two homes available to you. It can be made at any time in the two years beginning with the date from which it is to apply. You are, of course, free to vary it as and when it suits you.

If you own a home which was occupied rent free by the same dependent relative both on 5 April 1988 and throughout your period of ownership, then the profit on sale is tax free. Otherwise, it is likely that part of the gain will be taxable.

Chattels

Gains on the sales of chattels with an expected life of more than 50 years sold for less than £6,000 are exempt from tax. For items which fetch between £6,000 and £15,000 the chargeable gain is restricted to $^5/_3$ times the amount of the proceeds of sale (ignoring expenses) over £6,000 where this is to the taxpayer's advantage.

Illustration

A piece of antique furniture purchased in 1987 for £1,500 was sold in August 1997 for £9,000. Although the profit on sale was £7,500 the chargeable gain, ignoring the indexation allowance, is restricted to £5,000, being $^5/_3$ x (£9,000 − £6,000).

Where an article is sold at a loss for under £6,000, the allowable loss is restricted by assuming the proceeds on sale were equivalent to £6,000.

Illustration

A painting was purchased many years ago for £10,670. It subsequently transpired that it was a fake and was sold for £410. The loss on sale, ignoring the indexation allowance, is restricted to £4,670, being £10,670 less £6,000.

Articles comprising a set are regarded as a single item when they are sold to the same person but at different times.

Wasting assets

Wasting assets are assets with an expected life span of less than 50 years. Unless it comes within the definition of 'tangible moveable property' a gain on the sale of a wasting asset is calculated in the same way as that on the sale of any other asset, except that the purchase price wastes away during the asset's expected life span. Leases of land for less than 50 years are wasting assets. A specific table is provided for calculating the proportion of the purchase price of a lease which can be deducted from the sale proceeds.

The gain on a sale of a wasting asset which is also 'tangible moveable property' is exempt from tax. Neither does a loss on a sale of similar property count as an allowable loss.

Part disposals

Where you only sell part of an asset its acquisition cost is apportioned between the part sold and the proportion retained. This is done on a pro rata basis by reference to the proceeds of sale of the part sold and the open-market value of the proportion retained. The indexation allowance is calculated on the cost of the part sold. The proportion of the original cost of the asset attributable to the part which was not sold can be set against the proceeds on a sale of the remainder at a later date. This calculation must be reworked on the 31 March 1982 value of an asset acquired before that date where the part disposal took place before 6 April 1988.

If the part sold is small compared with the value of the entire asset or shareholding you can claim to deduct the sale proceeds from the acquisition cost. Where the part disposal is one of land this procedure can be adopted so long as the sale proceeds are both less than £20,000 and one fifth of the value of the remaining land.

Business assets

If you are in business and dispose of an asset used in your trade you have to pay Capital Gains Tax on the profit of sale. The profit or loss is calculated in the same way as that on a disposal of an asset you own personally. If the proceeds of sale are re-invested wholly or partly in other assets for use in the business, payment of the tax on the profit can be wholly or partly postponed by deducting the cost of the replacement assets from the capital gain realized on the disposal of the old asset.

When you come to dispose of your business assets on retirement either by sale or gift the first £250,000 and 50% of the next £750,000 of capital gains are exempt from tax. To qualify automatically for this maximum exemption you must have been in business for at least 10 years and be over age 50 at the time of the disposal. The same age qualification applies to both sexes. You can only claim this relief before age 50 if you retire prematurely owing to ill health.

The precise rules which apply in calculating the capital gain on the disposal of a business asset during the course of trading or on retirement are complicated. It is outside the scope of this book to go into them in detail. The indexation allowance features in both of them.

Reinvestment relief

All chargeable gains realized by individuals can be deferred if they are reinvested in eligible shares in unquoted trading companies. To qualify for this relief the chargeable gains must be reinvested within a period beginning one year before, and ending three years after, the original disposal. There is no requirement on the investor to take a minimum holding in the unquoted trading company. Tax on the original gain will remain deferred while the new shares are held. If, however, the unquoted trading company ceases to meet the qualifying conditions at any time within three years after the reinvestment is made, or if the shareholder emigrates within this three year period, then the deferred gain will be brought into charge to tax.

As with the previous section on business assets, the legislation dealing with reinvestment relief is lengthy. It contains a number of conditions and restrictions and is an area where you will inevitably need to seek professional advice.

Enterprise Investment Scheme

Any gain on the disposal of qualifying shares under the Scheme (see Chapter 10) is exempt from Capital Gains Tax providing the Income Tax relief on the investment has not been withdrawn. In addition, investors are allowed either Income Tax or Capital Gains Tax relief for losses made on the disposal of qualifying shares.

An investor can defer a chargeable gain arising on any disposal when that individual subscribes for shares under the Scheme. This must be made in a period beginning one year before, and ending three years after, the original disposal. In such circumstances, the investor subscribing for shares under the Enterprise Investment Scheme may qualify for total initial tax relief of up to 60%, comprising relief from Income Tax at 20% and, for a higher rate taxpayer, postponement of Capital Gains Tax at 40%. The deferred gain becomes taxable when the shares are sold or when certain other events occur.

Venture Capital Trusts

A disposal of shares in a Venture Capital Trust (see Chapter 10) will be free of Capital Gains Tax providing the original cost of the shares disposed of did not exceed £100,000 in any one tax year. For the profit on sale to qualify for relief from tax, the company must qualify as a Venture Capital Trust both at the time shares are acquired and also at the date of disposal.

Like Enterprise Investment Scheme shares a further relief is available for individuals who subscribe for new shares in a Venture Capital Trust, as opposed to purchase from a third party. Those individuals can defer a tax charge on a chargeable gain arising on the disposal of any assets providing the re-investment in new shares of a Venture Capital Trust is made in a period beginning one year before, and ending one year after, the original disposal. The relief is allowed, on the making of a claim, by deducting the amount of the investment in new shares from the chargeable gain. Tax on the deferred gain will be payable when the shares are sold or in certain other circumstances.

Gifts

The capital gain on a gift is calculated by using the market value of the asset at the date of gift. The amount of the gain is reduced by the indexation allowance which is due at the time.

Where the gift is one of business assets you can elect with the transferee for payment of the tax on the gift to be postponed until the asset is subsequently disposed of by the transferee. This same rule also applies in other restricted circumstances. For gifts of some assets where deferral is not available the Capital Gains Tax can be paid in 10 equal annual instalments.

Deferred gains on business assets and gifts

Earlier in this chapter you read about the rules for working out the capital gains on assets which you owned at the end of March 1982. In preceding sections I have made mention of postponing the payment of Capital Gains Tax on gifts and the proceeds of sale of business assets which are reinvested in other assets for use in the business.

Without some special form of relief, the benefit of these rules would be denied where a deferral occurred in the period from 31 March 1982 to 5 April 1988, and a charge to Capital Gains Taxes arises thereafter since the disposal is not of an asset owned on 31 March 1982. The remedy provides for a 50% reduction of the deferred gain.

Illustration

A business asset purchased in 1978 was sold in January 1986. The deferred gain on the sale was £56,000. The replacement asset cost £120,000 and was sold in May 1997 for £180,000. The indexation allowance between January 1986 and May 1997 is 0.630. The chargeable gain is £30,040 as follows:

	£	£
Sale proceeds		180,000
Less: Purchase price	120,000	
Less: Deferred gain	56,000	
	64,000	
Add: 50% of postponed gain	28,000	
	92,000	
Indexation allowance		
£92,000 × 0.630	57,960	149,960
1997/98 Chargeable gain		£30,040

Inheritances

No Capital Gains Tax is payable on the unrealized profits on your assets at the date of your death. When you inherit an asset you acquire it at the value on the date of death of the deceased. Generally, this rule is also applied whenever you become entitled to assets from a trust.

14

COMPLETING THE RETURN AND CALCULATING YOUR TAX

When you collect your post from the doormat you can always pick out your Tax Return from the other letters. It comes in a distinctive brown envelope at the same time every year. This book is being published at about the time you should be receiving your Tax Return asking for information on your income and capital gains for the year ended 5 April 1998. Everybody gets:

- the standard eight-page Return;

- guidance notes;

- supplementary pages based on his or her tax history;

- a tax calculation guide and working sheet.

There are also additional colour-coded supplementary pages specific to the income and gains of the taxpayer:

1. Employment	Pink
2. Share schemes	Purple
3. Self-employment	Orange
4. Partnership	Turquoise
5. Land and property	Red
6. Foreign income and gains and tax credit relief	Mustard
7. Trusts, settlements and the estates of deceased persons	Brown
8. Capital gains	Blue
9. Non-residence	Green

There are no supplementary pages for UK investment income which is entered on the main Return.

When you receive your Return try to avoid the temptation to put it to one side. Start by filling in page 2. This tells you which supplementary pages you will need. These can be obtained by telephoning the Orderline on 0645 000604 every day (apart from Christmas Day) from 8 a.m. to 10 p.m. You can also request any of the new Help Sheets by calling the same number:

IR 310	War Widow's and Dependants' Pension
IR 320	Gains on UK Life Insurance Policies
IR 325	Miscellaneous Other Income

IR 330   Pension Payments
IR 340   Non-MIRAS Loans
IR 350   Calculating Age Related Allowances
IR 201-213 Employment
IR 216-218 Share Schemes
IR 220-232 Self-Employment and Partnerships
IR 250-251 Land and Property
IR 260-263 Foreign
IR 270   Trusts
IR 280-301 Capital Gains

Then you should decide if you want to calculate your tax or if you want your Tax Office to do it for you. Remember the deadlines:

30 September 1998

You must send back your completed Tax Return for the year to 5 April 1998 to your Tax Office by then if you want the Inland Revenue to:

- calculate your tax in time for you to make payment on 31 January 1999; or

- collect tax owing of less than £1,000 through your tax code.

31 January 1999

This date is important for three reasons. By then you must:

- let your Tax Office have your completed Return;

- pay the balance of any tax you owe for the 1997/98 tax year (unless it is to be collected through your tax code); and

- if appropriate pay your first payment on account for the 1998/99 tax year.

You are now ready to complete the remainder of your Tax Return. Begin by gathering together all the information for the year ended 5 April 1998 on your income, capital gains, reliefs and allowances from the records you have been keeping for the year.

Keeping proper records

For most kinds of income and capital gains you will only need to keep the records given to you by whoever provided that income. This means for those of you

- in employment:

    your Form P60, a certificate your employer will give you after 5 April (the end of the tax year) showing details of pay and tax deducted;

118

any Form P45 (part 1A), a certificate from an employer showing details of pay and tax from a job you have left;

any Form P160 (part 1A) you may have been given when you retire and go on to receive a pension paid by your former employer;

your payslips or pay statements;

a note of the amount of any tips or gratuities and details of any other taxable receipts. You are advised to record these as soon as possible after you receive them, not simply estimate them at the end of the year;

Form P11D or P9D or equivalent information from all the employers you have worked for during the year, showing any benefits-in-kind and expenses payments given to you.

- receiving a UK pension or social security benefits:

  your Form P60, a certificate which may be given to you by the payer of your occupational pension, showing the amount of your pension and the tax deducted;

  any other certificate of a pension you received and the tax deducted from it;

  details given to you by either the Benefits Agency or the Employment Services Agency relating to state pensions, taxable state benefits, statutory sick pay, statutory maternity pay and the jobseeker's allowance.

- in business or letting property:

  please refer to Chapter 7 and the section on Records.

- receiving investment income:

  bank and building society statements or passbooks;

  statements of interest and any other income received from your savings and investments; for example, an annuity;

  any tax deduction certificates supplied by your bank or building society;

  dividend vouchers received from UK companies;

  unit trust tax vouchers;

  life insurance chargeable events certificate;

  details of any income you received from a trust.

It is also sensible to keep details of any exceptional amounts — such as an inheritance or other windfall — which you receive and invest.

- making capital gains or losses:

    contracts for the purchase or sale of shares, unit trusts, property or other assets;

    copies of any valuations taken into account in your calculation of capital gains or losses;

    bills, invoices or other evidence of payment records such as bank statements and cheque stubs for costs you claim for the purchase, improvement or sale of assets;

    details of any assets you have given away or put into a trust.

- claiming personal allowances, other deductions or reliefs:

    certificates of interest paid;

    court orders or other legally binding maintenance agreements;

    charitable deeds of covenant;

    personal pension plan and self-employed premium certificates;

    a birth certificate for any claim where age is relevant;

    a marriage certificate where the married couple's allowance is being claimed;

    a certificate of your husband's death if you are claiming the widow's bereavement allowance;

    notification that you registered as a blind person;

    evidence showing that a child over 16 years old is in full-time education or vocational training, if you are claiming the additional personal allowance in respect of that child.

These are some examples of the types of records you would be advised to keep. The list is not exhaustive and does not cover every situation. If you are in any doubt, ask your Tax Office or Tax Enquiry Centre for advice.

Even if you do not have all the information you need do not let this deter you from preparing your Tax Return and sending it back to your Tax Office. Of course, you must do all you can to get the information, but if you are unable to provide final figures when the time comes to send off your Tax Return then estimate the missing amounts. Tick box 22.3 on your Return and describe in the space provided:

- which figures are provisional. You should refer to the appropriate box numbers on your Tax Return or any of the other supplementary pages you have completed;

- why you could not give final figures;

- when you expect to be able to provide your Tax Office with the correct information.

Your Tax Office will not normally regard a Tax Return as incomplete just because it contains provisional details of income or capital gains provided you have taken all reasonable measures to obtain the final figures, and you make sure that you send them as soon as they are available.

Completing the Return

You must answer all the questions. If you tick the 'No' box then move on to the next question. If you answer 'Yes' you should fill in the boxes which apply to you.

Always

- write only in the space provided using blue or black ink;

- only use numbers when you are asked for amounts;

- do not include pence.

There is just not enough space for me to reproduce all the supplementary pages and the core Tax Return in the Guide. I have therefore decided to reproduce the front of the supplementary page on Employment and most of pages 3 to 8 of the Tax Return.

If you have more than one job you will need to fill in a separate copy of the Employment page for each employment. In box 1.8 enter your before-tax salary or wage from your form P60. Put the tax deducted by your employer in box 1.11. The amounts of any benefits-in-kind, which are taxable, will have been worked out by your employer and can be clearly identified from the copy of your form P11D which will be given to you. Enter these benefits and expenses, if appropriate, in boxes 1.12 to 1.23. The reverse of the employment page deals with:

- lump sums and compensation payments;

- foreign earnings;

- expenses you incurred in doing your job.

Income for the year ended 5 April 1998

Revenue inland

EMPLOYMENT

Name

Fill in these boxes first

ROGER FLYNN

Tax reference

28739 68720

If you want help, look up the box numbers in the Notes

Details of employer

Employer's PAYE reference

1.1 195 ⌗ 249

Employer's name

1.2 FIELDGATE TEXTILE CO. LTD

Date employment started
(only if between 6 April 1997 and 5 April 1998)

1.3 / /

Date finished (only if between 6 April 1997 and 5 April 1998)

1.4 / /

Employer's address

1.5 FLOWERS LANE

FIELDGATE

Postcode TA6 5NZ

Tick box 1.6 if you were a director of the company

1.6

and, if so, tick box 1.7 if it was a close company

1.7

Income from employment

Money *- see Notes, page EN3*

Before tax

- Payments from P60 (or P45 or pay slips)

1.8 £ 24,000

- Payments not on P60 etc.   - tips

1.9 £

  - other payments (excluding expenses shown below and lump sums and compensation payments or benefits shown overleaf)

1.10 £

- Tax deducted from payments in boxes 1.8 to 1.10

Tax deducted

1.11 £ 5,123 - 65

Benefits and expenses *- see Notes, pages EN3 to EN6*

	Amount			Amount
• Assets transferred/ payments made for you	**1.12** £		• Vans	**1.18** £
• Vouchers/credit cards	**1.13** £		• Interest-free and low-interest loans	**1.19** £
• Living accommodation	**1.14** £		• Mobile telephones	**1.20** £
• Mileage allowance	**1.15** £		• Private medical or dental insurance	**1.21** £ 360
• Company cars	**1.16** £ 2,680		• Other benefits	**1.22** £
• Fuel for company cars	**1.17** £ 1,010		• Expenses payments received and balancing charges	**1.23** £

SA101

BMSD 12/97

TAX RETURN EMPLOYMENT: PAGE E1

Please turn over

If you received income from UK savings and investments tick the 'Yes' box at the top of page 3 of your Tax Return. You then need to complete boxes 10.1 to 10.32 as appropriate. The page is divided into two halves:

- interest

  Take note that there are two lines which specifically deal with interest you have received from UK banks, building societies or National Savings where no tax has been deducted.

- dividends

  Dividends on your shareholdings come with counterfoils. These show the amount of the dividend and the accompanying tax credit. It is the total of all of your dividends in the year, and tax credits, which should be entered in boxes 10.15 and 10.16. Add these totals together to get the 'dividend/distribution plus credit' figure to be shown in box 10.17. The same procedure should be followed for all other dividends which you have received including those on your unit trust investments and 'scrip' dividends from UK companies. A 'scrip' dividend is where you take up an offer of shares instead of a cash dividend.

INCOME *for the year ended 5 April 1998*

Q 10 **Did you receive any income from UK savings and investments?** NO YES ✓ *If yes, fill in boxes 10.1 to 10.32 as appropriate. Include only your share from any joint savings and investments.*

■ *Interest*

● Interest from UK banks, building societies and deposit takers

			Taxable amount
- where no tax has been deducted			**10.1** £

	Amount after tax deducted	Tax deducted	Gross amount before tax
- where tax has been deducted	**10.2** £ 192	**10.3** £ 48	**10.4** £ 240

● Interest distributions from UK authorised unit trusts and open-ended investment companies (dividend distributions go below)	Amount after tax deducted	Tax deducted	Gross amount before tax
	10.5 £	**10.6** £	**10.7** £

● National Savings (other than FIRST Option Bonds and the first £70 of interest from a National Savings Ordinary Account)			Taxable amount
			10.8 £ 350

● National Savings FIRST Option Bonds	Amount after tax deducted	Tax deducted	Gross amount before tax
	10.9 £ 112	**10.10** £ 28	**10.11** £ 140

● Other income from UK savings and investments (except dividends)	Amount after tax deducted	Tax deducted	Gross amount before tax
	10.12 £	**10.13** £	**10.14** £

■ *Dividends*

● Dividends and other qualifying distributions from UK companies	Dividend/distribution	Tax credit	Dividend/distribution plus credit
	10.15 £ 276	**10.16** £ 69	**10.17** £ 345

● Dividend distributions from UK authorised unit trusts and open-ended investment companies	Dividend/distribution	Tax credit	Dividend/distribution plus credit
	10.18 £ 132	**10.19** £ 33	**10.20** £ 165

● Scrip dividends from UK companies	Dividend	Notional tax	Dividend plus notional tax
	10.21 £ 32	**10.22** £ 8	**10.23** £ 40

● Foreign income dividends from UK companies	Dividend	Notional tax	Dividend plus notional tax
	10.24 £	**10.25** £	**10.26** £

● Foreign income dividend distributions from UK authorised unit trusts and open-ended investment companies	Dividend	Notional tax	Dividend plus notional tax
	10.27 £	**10.28** £	**10.29** £

● Non-qualifying distributions and loans written off		Notional tax	Taxable amount
	10.30 £	**10.31** £	**10.32** £

124

Did you receive a UK pension, retirement annuity or social security benefit in 1997/98. If your pension or benefit is taxable and should be included on the Return tick the 'Yes' box at the top of page 4 and fill in boxes 11.1 to 11.12, as appropriate. As with the Employment page the amount of your pension from a previous employer's pension fund, and the tax deducted throughout the year, will also be shown on a form P60 which has been sent to you. If you are drawing the state pension you should declare the amount of your pension for the 52-week period to 5 April 1998. Particularly where the pension is paid quarterly, there will be a small difference between the income you should declare on the Return and the actual pension received during the tax year. Do not include the £10 Christmas Bonus as this is not taxable.

INCOME *for the year ended 5 April 1998, continued*

Q11 Did you receive a UK pension, retirement annuity or Social Security benefit?   NO [ ]   YES [✓]   If yes, fill in boxes 11.1 to 11.13 as appropriate.

■■ *State pensions and benefits*   Taxable amount for 1997-98

● State Retirement Pension	**11.1** £ 3,247
● Widow's Pension	**11.2** £
● Widowed Mother's Allowance	**11.3** £
● Industrial Death Benefit Pension	**11.4** £
● Jobseeker's Allowance	**11.5** £
● Invalid Care Allowance	**11.6** £
● Statutory Sick Pay and Statutory Maternity Pay paid by the Department of Social Security	**11.7** £

	Tax deducted	Gross amount before tax
● Taxable Incapacity Benefit	**11.8** £	**11.9** £

Other pensions and retirement annuities

	Amount after tax deducted	Tax deducted	Gross amount before tax
● Pensions (other than State pensions) and retirement annuities	**11.10** £ 4,437	**11.11** £ 616	**11.12** £ 5,053

	Amount of deduction	
● Deduction - see the note for box 11.3 on page 14 of your Tax Return Guide	**11.13** £	

Question 12 will only be of any concern to you if you received any of the following kinds of income:

- taxable maintenance or alimony;

- gains on UK life insurance policies, life annuities or capital redemption policies;

- refunds of surplus additional voluntary contributions.

If you tick the 'No' box you can go straight to question 13 which asks you whether you received any other income which has not already been entered elsewhere on your Tax Return. This would include, for example:

- any casual earnings not declared elsewhere;

- accrued income on a transfer of securities;

- income received after your business has ceased.

Question 14 is the first in the section dealing with reliefs for the year ended 5 April 1998 and is relevant if you want to claim relief for pension contributions. If:

- you pay into both a retirement annuity contract and a personal pension plan; or

- you bring back into 1997/98 payments made after 5 April 1998; or

- you carry back payments in 1997/98 to a previous year; or

- the figure in box 14.5, or 14.10, or 14.15 is more than the appropriate percentage limit of your earnings;

you must telephone the Orderline and ask for Help Sheet IR 330 Pension Payments which includes working sheets to help you complete the boxes.

RELIEFS for the year ended 5 April 1998

Q14 Do you want to claim relief for pension contributions? NO ☐ YES ✓   If yes, fill in boxes 14.1 to 14.17 as appropriate.

Do not include contributions deducted from your pay by your employer to their pension scheme, because tax relief is given automatically. But do include your contributions to personal pension schemes.

■ Retirement annuity contracts

Qualifying payments made in 1997-98	14.1 £ 1,100	1997-98 payments used in an earlier year	14.2 £
1997-98 payments now to be carried back	14.3 £	Payments brought back from 1998-99	14.4 £

Relief claimed
box 14.1 *minus* (boxes 14.2 and 14.3, but not 14.4)
14.5 £ 1,100

■ Self-employed contributions to personal pension plans

Qualifying payments made in 1997-98	14.6 £ 1,250	1997-98 payments used in an earlier year	14.7 £
1997-98 payments now to be carried back	14.8 £	Payments brought back from 1998-99	14.9 £

Relief claimed
box 14.6 *minus* (boxes 14.7 and 14.8, but not 14.9)
14.10 £ 1,250

■ Employee contributions to personal pension plans (include your gross contribution - see the note on box 14.11 in your Tax Return Guide)

Qualifying payments made in 1997-98	14.11 £	1997-98 payments used in an earlier year	14.12 £
1997-98 payments now to be carried back	14.13 £	Payments brought back from 1998-99	14.14 £

Relief claimed
box 14.11 *minus* (boxes 14.12 and 14.13, but not 14.14)
14.15 £

■ Contributions to other pension schemes

- Amount of contributions to employer's schemes **not deducted** at source from pay   14.16 £
- Gross amount of free-standing additional voluntary contributions paid in 1997-98   14.17 £

Question 15 lists a number of reliefs. Do you want to claim any of them? They include interest on a loan to buy your main home. In most cases a loan to buy your home is eligible for mortgage interest relief at source (MIRAS). You get relief by paying only the net amount of interest to the lender. If your home loan is in MIRAS, no more information is required by your Tax Office and you do not need to complete box 15.2. Other reliefs listed include:

- payments for vocational training;

- interest on qualifying loans;

- maintenance or alimony payments you are making;

- your subscriptions for new ordinary shares in a Venture Capital Trust;

- subscriptions under the Enterprise Investment Scheme;

- your annual covenanted payments to charities;

- your donations under Gift Aid.

| Q 15 | Do you want to claim any of the following reliefs? | NO | YES ✓ | If yes, fill in boxes 15.1 to 15.12, as appropriate |

	Amount of payment
● Payments you made for vocational training	**15.1** £
● Interest on loans to buy your main home (other than MIRAS)	**15.2** £
● Interest on other qualifying loans	**15.3** £ 624

	Amount claimed under 'new' rules	
● Maintenance or alimony payments you have made under a court order, Child Support Agency assessment or legally binding order or agreement	**15.4** £	

Amount claimed under 'old' rules up to £1,830	Amount claimed under 'old' rules over £1,830
15.5 £	**15.6** £ 2,210

	Amount on which relief claimed
● Subscriptions for Venture Capital Trust shares (up to £100,000)	**15.7** £ 3,000
● Subscriptions under the Enterprise Investment Scheme (up to £100,000)	**15.8** £

	Amount of payment
● Charitable covenants or annuities	**15.9** £ 25
● Gift Aid	**15.10** £ 800
● Post-cessation expenses and losses on relevant discounted securities etc.	**15.11** £

	Half amount of payment
● Payments to a trade union or friendly society for death benefits	**15.12** £

The whole of page 6, and indeed question 16, is devoted to the allowances for the year ended 5 April 1998 which you may want to claim. There are separate sections covering all the personal allowances and the individuals – whether they be single, married, young or old – who can claim them. In each case there is a space for you to enter the information the Inland Revenue need to make sure you are given the full and right tax allowances.

The first part of this section is for you to make a claim for the special blind person's allowance. You will need to give the name of the local authority, or equivalent body, with whom you have registered your blindness as well as the date of registration.

Then follows a reference to the transitional allowance for some wives with husbands on low income if claimed in earlier years. This section is likely to be of limited application.

Then come sections on the married couple's allowance – the first if you are a married man and the second if you are a married woman. A man can claim the married couple's allowance if he is married and lives with his wife for all or part of the tax year. There are also spaces on the Return to enter the date of your marriage, if after 5 April 1997, and to deal with the allocation of the married couple's allowance between husband and wife.

ALLOWANCES *for the year ended 5 April 1998*

Q 16 ▶ You get your personal allowance of £4,045 automatically. **If you were born before 6 April 1933, enter your date of birth in box 21.4 - you may get higher age-related allowances.**

Do you want to claim any of the following allowances?   NO [ ]   YES [✓]

If yes, please read pages 23 to 26 of your Tax Return Guide and then fill in boxes 16.1 to 16.28 as appropriate.

	Date of registration (if first year of claim)		Local authority (or other register)
■ *Blind person's allowance*	16.1	23 / 05 / 91	16.2 TOPMARSH COUNTY COUNCIL

■ *Transitional allowance* (for some wives with husbands on low income if claimed in earlier years)

- Tick to claim and give details in the 'Additional information' box on page 8 *(please see page 23 of your Tax Return Guide for what is needed)* 16.3 [ ]

- If you want to calculate your tax, enter the amount of transitional allowance you can have in box 16.4 16.4 £ [ ]

■ *Married couple's allowance for a married man* - see page 23 of your Tax Return Guide.

- Wife's full name 16.5 WENDY MARTIN
  - Date of marriage (if after 5 April 1997) 16.6 26 / 07 / 97

- Wife's date of birth (if before 6 April 1933) 16.7 / /
  - Tick box 16.8 if you or your wife have allocated half the allowance to her 16.8 [ ]

- Wife's tax reference (if known, please) 16.9 210 / T634
  - Tick box 16.10 if you and your wife have allocated all the allowance to her 16.10 [ ]

■ *Married couple's allowance for a married woman* - see page 24 of your Tax Return Guide.

  - Date of marriage (if after 5 April 1997) 16.11 26 / 07 / 97

- Husband's full name 16.12 TONY MARTIN
  - Tick box 16.13 if you or your husband have allocated half the allowance to you 16.13 [ ]

- Husband's tax reference (if known, please) 16.14 195 / P482
  - Tick box 16.15 if you and your husband have allocated all the allowance to you 16.15 [ ]

You can claim an additional personal allowance if you have a child and are single, separated, divorced or widowed. The conditions which need to be satisfied before this allowance can be claimed are not identical for men and women. There are also special rules for unmarried couples living together. A widow with a child living with her at home will complete this part of her Tax Return as follows:

■ *Additional personal allowance (available in some circumstances if you have a child living with you - see page 24 of your Tax Return Guide).*

• Name of the child claimed for **16.16** PATRICIA SMITH

• Child's date of birth **16.17** 16 / 12 / 79

• Tick if child lives with you **16.18**

• Name of university etc/type of training if the child is 16 or over on 6 April 1997 and in full time education or training **16.19** FIELDGATE TECHNICAL COLLEGE

Sharing a claim
Name and address of other person claiming

16.20

Postcode

• Enter your share as a percentage **16.21** %
• If share not agreed, enter the number of days in the year ended 5 April 1998 that the child lived with

  - you **16.22** days
  - other person **16.23** days

Widows may be entitled to the widow's bereavement allowance. You can claim this in the tax year in which your husband died and also the following tax year. Enter the date of your husband's death to make your claim.

■ *Widow's bereavement allowance*   • Date of your husband's death **16.24** 10 / 04 / 97

Finally, at the bottom of page 6 there is a section on the transfer of surplus allowances to your wife or husband.

The final two pages of the Return ask for other information for the year ended 5 April 1998 and are all relatively straightforward. When the Return is finished it must be signed and dated in the space provided on the back page. Bear in mind the wording of the declaration: 'The information I have given in this Tax Return is correct and complete to the best of my knowledge and belief'. Then send the form back to your Tax Office. As there is no space in each section of the Return you may well need to prepare separate statements of, for example, your interest and dividend income in order to arrive at the single figures which need to be entered on the Return. I strongly recommend that copies of any supporting statements or schedules which you prepare should be sent to your Tax Office along with the Return. Do not, however, send in any building society statements, dividend vouchers and other financial records. Just keep them safely.

If, after you have sent off your Tax Return, you find that you have made a mistake, let your Tax Office know at once so that it can be taken into account.

Calculating your Tax

You should receive a Tax Calculation Guide with your Tax Return. This will help you if you want to calculate your tax. The key steps in calculating your tax bill are as follows:

- work out your total taxable income for 1997/98;

- deduct reliefs from that income;

- calculate the Income Tax due taking account of allowances and reliefs given in terms of tax;

- add other amounts due (for example, Class 4 National Insurance Contributions and any unpaid tax for earlier years);

- deduct any 1997/98 tax already paid or accounted for;

- work out what you owe taking account of any payments on account for 1997/98 and adjustments for earlier years;

- work out if you need to make payments on account for 1998/99;

- work out what you need to pay.

The working sheet in the middle of the Tax Calculation Guide will take you through these steps.

Illustration

George Salmon is employed by a local company as a senior engineer. Since the beginning of July 1994 he has regularly been asked to speak at seminars and write articles for trade magazines. George is 53 (he was born on 8 February 1945) and is happily married to Lynne. He owns a modest number of investments and his spare cash is deposited in National Savings and building society accounts.

George files his Tax Return for the year to 5 April 1998 on 11 November 1998. It shows the following entries:

	£	Box Number in Return
(1) *Employment*		
Salary	35,000.00	1.8
Tax deducted by employer	9,391.50	1.11
Subscription to the Association of Mechanical Engineers	100.00	1.34
Company car benefit	3,700.00	1.16
Fuel benefit for company car	1,010.00	1.17

	£	Box Number in Return

(2) Self-Employment

Adjusted profit shown by the accounts
for the year to 30 June 1997 — 8,000.00 — 3.88

George applied for, and was granted,
permission to defer payment of Class 4
National Insurance Contributions

Tax payments of £1,000 have been
made on both 31 January 1998 and
31 July 1998 based on George's tax
liability for 1996/97

Personal pension premiums paid in 1997/98
(including unused relief from earlier years
of £100) — 2,500.00 — 14.6
& 14.10

(3) Savings Income

	£	
National Savings Income Bonds (paid gross)	250.00	10.8
Building Society interest received		
– gross interest	600.00	10.4
tax deducted	120.00	10.3
net interest	480.00	10.2
Dividends from share investments		
– gross	1,500.00	10.17
tax credit	300.00	10.16
dividends	1,200.00	10.15

(4) Reliefs

In the year George paid £308 (equivalent
to £400 before tax) under Gift Aid to
the Cancer Research Campaign — 15.10

George will fill in his tax calculation working sheet as follows:

Tax Calculation Working Sheet

► Total income from: (copy figures from your Tax Return)

- **Employment** *including* benefits and *minus* expenses for **each** employment

	First employment	Other employments	If any of the sums on this page result in a negative amount, enter a zero in the appropriate box
Add income in boxes 1.8 to 1.10, 1.12 to 1.23, 1.27 and 1.28	£ 39,710	£	
Deduct any figures in boxes 1.31 to 1.38	£ 100	£	
Total taxable income	£ 39,610	+ £	= W1 £ 39,610

- **Share schemes** (from box 2.31) — W2 £
- **Self-employment** (from box 3.88) — W3 £ 8,000
- **Partnerships** (from boxes 4.35, 4.70 and 4.73) — W4 £
- **UK land and property** (from box 5.43) — W5 £
- **Foreign income** (from boxes 6.2, 6.4 and 6.5) — W6 £
- **Trusts, settlements or estates of deceased persons** (add together any figures in the 'right hand' column of the Trusts etc Pages and deduct any figure in box 7.19) — W7 £
- **UK savings and investments** (total any figures in the 'right hand' column on page 3 of your Tax Return) — W8 £ 2,350
- **UK pensions, retirement annuities and benefits** (add together any figures in the 'right hand' column of Question 11 on page 4 of your Tax Return *minus* any deduction in box 11.13) — W9 £
- **Maintenance and alimony received** (from box 12.3) — W10 £
- **Other income** (copy the figure in box 13.3 minus any figure in box 13.5) — W11 £

Total column above

Total W12 £ 49,960

► Deductions for

- **Personal pension** (add together any figures in boxes 14.5, 14.10, 14.15, 14.16 and 14.17) — W13 £ 2,500
- **Vocational training** (multiply any figure in box 15.1 by $^{100}/_{77}$) — W14 £
- **Interest on qualifying loans** (from box 15.3) — W15 £
- **Maintenance or alimony paid** (see the notes on page 2 of this Guide) — W16 £
- **Charitable covenants, annuities and Gift Aid payments** (multiply any figures in boxes 15.9 and 15.10 by $^{100}/_{77}$) — W17 £ 400
- **Losses and post-cessation expenses** (from boxes 3.81, 4.15, 4.61, 5.16, 5.44, 8.13A and 15.11) — W18 £
- **Trade union and friendly society death benefit payments** (from box 15.12) — W19 £

Total boxes W13 to W19

Total W20 £ 2,900

► Total income minus deductions

box W12 *minus* box W20

W21 £ 47,060

■ TAX CALCULATION GUIDE: PAGE 5

now copy the figure in box W21 to box W22 on page 7

Tax Calculation Working Sheet continued

Reliefs
- you get basic rate relief automatically - further relief will be due if you are liable to higher rate tax.

- **Pension payments**
  (from boxes 14.15 and 14.17) — W23.1 £

- **Vocational training**
  (from box W14) — W23.2 £

Total W23.3 £

Fill in any boxes on this page that apply to you and copy to page 7. Then work through remaining boxes on pages 7 and 8

Copy to W23

Allowances given as a deduction from your income
- you may need to check your entitlement - see notes, page 3.

- **Personal allowance**
  - normally £4,045 unless you are non-resident and not claiming allowances — W25.1 £ 4,045

- **Age-related personal allowance**
  - see notes page 3 — W25.2 £

Savings income taxable at the lower (20%) rate.

- **Partnership savings**
  (from boxes 4.35 and 4.70) — W28.1 £

- **UK savings**
  (from box W8) — W28.2 £ 2,350

- **Foreign savings**
  (from box 6.2) — W28.3 £

- **Trusts, settlements and estate income**
  (from boxes 7.6, 7.12 and 7.15) — W28.4 £

Total W28.5 £

- **Blind person's allowance**
  - enter £1,280 — W25.3 £

- **Transitional allowance**
  (from box 16.4) — W25.4 £

- **Blind person's surplus allowance from your spouse**
  (from box 16.27) — W25.5 £

Total W25.6 £ 4,045

Copy to W28

Allowances and reliefs given in terms of tax
- these reduce your tax bill - you may need to use the Question 16 notes on pages 23 to 26 of the Tax Return Guide and starting on page 3 of this Guide.

- **Married couple's allowance**
  - see notes, pages 4 and 9 — W42.1 £ 1,830

- **Married couple's surplus allowance**
  (from box 16.28) — W42.2 £

- **Additional personal allowance**
  - usually £1,830, may be split with another person - see the notes — W42.3 £

Notional tax is not repayable and so has to be calculated as an allowance given in terms of tax rather than being regarded as tax deducted at source.

- **Partnership notional tax**
  (from box 4.78) — W44.1 £

- **Notional tax on UK scrip dividends and FIDs** (from boxes 10.22, 10.25, 10.28 and 10.31) — W44.2 £

- **Notional tax on estate income** (from box 7.14) — W44.3 £

Total W44.4 £

- **Widow's bereavement allowance - £1,830**
  (if your husband died in 1996-97 or 1997-98 and you have not remarried) — W42.4 £

- **Interest on home loans (other than MIRAS)** (from box 15.2) — W42.5 £

- **Maintenance and alimony**
  (boxes 15.4 and 15.5 - see the notes for box W16) — W42.6 £

Total W42.7 £ 1,830

Copy to W44

x Calculation Working Sheet continued

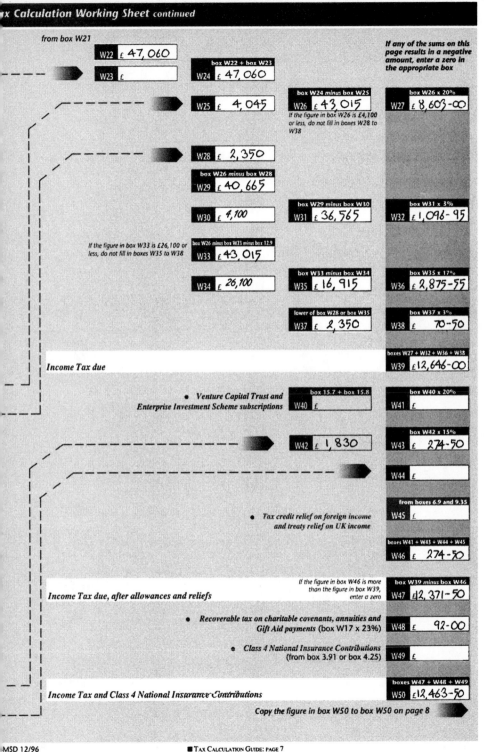

from box W21

W22 £ 47,060

W23 £

box W22 + box W23
W24 £ 47,060

If any of the sums on this page results in a negative amount, enter a zero in the appropriate box

W25 £ 4,045

box W24 minus box W25
W26 £ 43,015
If the figure in box W26 is £4,100 or less, do not fill in boxes W28 to W38

box W26 x 20%
W27 £ 8,603-00

W28 £ 2,350

box W26 minus box W28
W29 £ 40,665

W30 £ 4,100

box W29 minus box W30
W31 £ 36,565

box W31 x 3%
W32 £ 1,096-95

If the figure in box W33 is £26,100 or less, do not fill in boxes W35 to W38

box W26 minus box W23 minus box 12.9
W33 £ 43,015

W34 £ 26,100

box W33 minus box W34
W35 £ 16,915

box W35 x 17%
W36 £ 2,875-55

lower of box W28 or box W35
W37 £ 2,350

box W37 x 3%
W38 £ 70-50

Income Tax due

boxes W27 + W32 + W36 + W38
W39 £12,646-00

• **Venture Capital Trust and Enterprise Investment Scheme subscriptions**

box 15.7 + box 15.8
W40 £

box W40 x 20%
W41 £

W42 £ 1,830

box W42 x 15%
W43 £ 274-50

W44 £

• **Tax credit relief on foreign income and treaty relief on UK income**

from boxes 6.9 and 9.35
W45 £

boxes W41 + W43 + W44 + W45
W46 £ 274-50

Income Tax due, after allowances and reliefs

If the figure in box W46 is more than the figure in box W39, enter a zero

box W39 minus box W46
W47 £12,371-50

• **Recoverable tax on charitable covenants, annuities and Gift Aid payments (box W17 x 23%)**
W48 £ 92-00

• **Class 4 National Insurance Contributions (from box 3.91 or box 4.25)**
W49 £

Income Tax and Class 4 National Insurance Contributions

boxes W47 + W48 + W49
W50 £12,463-50

Copy the figure in box W50 to box W50 on page 8

Tax Calculation Working Sheet continued

Income Tax and Class 4 NIC due (from box W50 on page 7)

	W50 £12,463-50
	box W50 + box W51
• Unpaid tax for earlier years included in PAYE code for 1997-98	W51 £
	W52 £12,463-50

Copy box W51 above to box 18.1 in your Tax Return

Tax paid at source

- **Employment** (from boxes 1.11 and 1.30) — W53.1 £ 9,391-50
- **Self-employment** (from box 3.92) — W53.2 £
- **Partnerships** (from box 4.77) — W53.3 £
- **UK land and property** (from box 5.21) — W53.4 £
- **Foreign income** (from boxes 6.1 and 6.3) — W53.5 £
- **Trusts, settlements or estate income** (from boxes 7.2, 7.5, 7.8 and 7.11) — W53.6 £
- **UK savings** (from boxes 10.3, 10.6, 10.10, 10.13, 10.16 and 10.19) — W53.7 £ 420-00
- **UK pensions, retirement annuities and benefits** (from boxes 11.8 and 11.11) — W53.8 £
- **Other income** (from box 13.2) — W53.9 £

Total W53.10 £ 9,811-50

W53 £ 9,811-50
Copy to box W53

- Tax due for 1997-98 included in the 1998-99 PAYE tax code — W54 £
Copy to box 18.2 in your Tax Return

box W53 + box W54
W55 £9,811-50

box W52 minus box W55
W56 £ 2,652-00
Copy box W56 to box 18.3 in your Tax Return

Total tax and Class 4 NIC due for 1997-98 (overpayment in brackets)

Tax owed or overpaid in 1997-98

- 1997-98 tax already refunded (from box 17.1) — W57A £
- Tax due for earlier years — W57 £
  Copy box W57 to box 18.4 in your Tax Return

box WS6 + box W57A + box W57
W58 £ 2,652-00

- Tax overpaid for earlier years — W59 £
  Tick box 18.5 and copy this figure to the 'Additional information' box on page 8 of your Tax Return

- Payments already made — W60 £ 2,000-00
  (from your Statements of Account)

box W59 + box W60
W61 £ 2,000-00

Tax you owe for 1997-98
box W58 minus box W61
W62 £ 652-00

OR

Tax you have overpaid for 1997-98
box W61 minus box W58
W63 £

Payments on account for 1998-99

Copy W62 to W64 if it is less than £1,000 and you would like the amount you owe collected through your 1999-2000 tax code. Otherwise enter zero
W64 £

If W65 is **less** than £500, you do not need to make payments on account. Leave box 18.6 blank and tick box 18.8 your Tax Return.
If W65 is equal to or more than £500, carry on

box W56 minus box W64
W65 £2,652-00

- Income Tax due, after allowances and reliefs — **from boxes W47 + W44 + W48** W66 £12,463-50

box W66 + box W67
W68 £12,463-50

box W68 x 20%
W69 £ 2,492-70

- Class 4 National Insurance Contributions — **from box W49** W67 £

If W65 is **less** than W69, you do not need to make payments on account. Leave box 18.6 blank and tick box 18.8.
If it is equal to or **more** than W69, you do have to make payments on account. Fill in box W70.

This is the amount of each payment on account for 1998-99
box W65 x 50%
W70 £ 1,326-00
Copy box W70 (including pence) to box 18.6 in your Tax Return

From his tax calculation working sheet George will then be able to fill in question 18 of his Tax Return as follows:

Q 18	**Do you want to calculate your tax?**	NO	YES ✓	If yes, do it now and then fill in boxes 18.1 to 18.9. Your Tax Calculation Guide will help.
•	Unpaid tax for earlier years included in your tax code for 1997-98		18.1 £	
•	Tax due for 1997-98 included in your tax code for a later year		18.2 £	
•	Total tax and Class 4 NIC due for 1997-98 *(put the amount in brackets if an overpayment)*		18.3 £ *2,652·00*	
•	Tax due for earlier years		18.4 £	
•	Tick box 18.5 if you have calculated tax overpaid for earlier years (and enter the amount in the 'Additional information' box on page 8)		18.5	
•	Your first payment on account for 1998-99 *(include the pence)*		18.6 £ *1,326·00*	
	Tick box 18.7 if you are making a claim to reduce your payments on account and say why in the 'Additional information' box **18.7**	Tick box 18.8 if you do not need to make payments on account	18.8	
•	1998-99 tax you are reclaiming now		18.9 £	

What the Inland Revenue does

When your completed Tax Return is received by your Tax Office it will be processed as quickly as possible based on your figures, to sort out how much tax you owe, or how much tax is due back to you from the Inland Revenue. Any simple mistakes will be corrected right away and you will be told about them. This may simply be because your figures do not add up.

You will be sent a calculation of your tax position if you have asked the Inland Revenue to do it for you. If you have worked out your own tax bill, and it is wrong, you will also be advised of the mistakes you have made.

Once your Tax Return has been processed it will be checked. The Inland Revenue have 12 months from 31 January 1999 to check your Tax Return for the year ended 5 April 1998 (longer if you are late in submitting your Return). Remember that enquiries may be made into your figures and you may be asked by your Tax Office to send in your records in support of them.

15

TAX PAYMENTS, INTEREST, SURCHARGES AND PENALTIES

By now I am sure you have appreciated that much of the previous tax system, such as PAYE on wages and salaries, continues under Self-Assessment. But two further features of the new regime are:

- one set of payment dates for tax not paid at source;

- a clear statement of your 'account' with the Inland Revenue, showing tax payments both made and due.

Tax Payments

Every taxpayer with tax to pay on his or her Self-Assessment must pay the tax due by 31 January following the end of the tax year covered by the Return.

Some taxpayers – mainly the self-employed – will also make two payments on account for the tax year before the Return for that year needs to be submitted. These payments on account are due on:

- 31 January in the tax year; and

- 31 July following the end of the tax year.

If you work out your own tax you will also calculate your own payments on account. Normally you will split into two equal parts the tax paid in the previous tax year (after taking off tax paid at source and any Capital Gains Tax) and pay one half on 31 January and the second instalment six months later at the end of July. However, if you ask your Tax Office to work out your tax then they will also let you know if you have to make payments on account, and for how much.

You will not need to make payments on account:

- if your liability to Income Tax and Class 4 National Insurance Contributions for the previous tax year – after deducting tax suffered at source on, for example, dividends and Building Society interest – is less than £500; or

- if more than 80% of your liability to Income Tax and Class 4 National Insurance Contributions for the previous tax year was satisfied by tax paid at source;

- for Capital Gains Tax.

These tests mean that most employees and pensioners who complete Returns will not have to make payments on account under Self-Assessment. Instead such taxpayers will simply:

- have to make the one balancing payment on 31 January after the end of the tax year; or

- have the balancing payment collected through an adjustment to their PAYE coding.

Perhaps, because of a change in your circumstances, the calculation of your payments on account for the year (based, of course, on your tax liability for the previous year) seems likely to overstate your liability for the year. You can then claim to reduce your payments on account. This should be done by using form SA303 which is available from any Tax Office. The form also gives you guidance on how to fill it in. When completed, send it back to your Tax Office.

If your claim to reduce your payments on account subsequently turns out to be excessive then you will be asked to pay interest on the difference between the tax actually paid to the Collector of Taxes and the amounts that should have been paid.

The tax payment dates for 1997/98 are:

		Due date for Tax Payments on Account		Due date for Final Balance
Rental income and untaxed investment income				
Business profits		50%	31/01/98	31/01/99
Underpaid PAYE (where not coded)		50%	31/07/98	
Higher Rate Tax on investment income (taxed at source)				
Capital Gains Tax			N/A	31/01/99

Statements of Account

Under Self-Assessment taxpayers will get statements showing their account with the Inland Revenue. As well as including a payslip the statements set out tax to be paid as well as amounts that have been paid. If you are making payments on account you can expect to receive the following statements up to February 1999:

July 1998	To remind you of the second payment on account for 1997/98 due on 31 July.
August 1998	To tell you of any outstanding balance of the second payment on account. The statement will also include an amount for interest due to date.
January 1999	To advise you of your balancing payment for 1997/98 and your first payment on account for 1998/99, both due on 31 January 1999.
February 1999	To show any outstanding amounts of your Self-Assessment for 1997/98 and your first payment on account for 1998/99. The statement will also include a charge for interest due to date.

Taxpayers who do not need to make payments on account will not, of course, receive so many statements of account from their Tax Office. If you are late in paying your tax you will receive additional statements each month.

Interest

If you delay paying your tax you will be charged interest. This applies to both payments on account and balancing payments. The rate of interest is worked out on a set formula. It is an average of the base rates of six main banks (rounded to the nearest whole number) plus 2.5%. At the time of going into print the rate is 9.5%. The interest is calculated from the due date up until payment. You cannot claim tax relief on the interest.

You will be paid interest on any overpayments of tax. The interest, called repayment supplement, is not taxable. The rate of interest is worked out by first of all taking 1% off the average base rate mentioned above. The resulting figure is then further reduced by the 20% rate of Income Tax deducted at source from investment income. At the time of going into print the rate of repayment supplement is 4.75%.

Surcharges

With Self-Assessment come surcharges. They will be levied automatically on late payment of Capital Gains Tax or the final amount of Income Tax owing as follows:

Tax unpaid by 28 February (1 month after the tax was due)	5% of unpaid tax
Tax unpaid by 31 July (6 months after the tax was due)	Further 5% of tax unpaid

Notice of any surcharge must be served on you formally by the Inland Revenue. You do have the right to appeal within 30 days if you think

140

you have a reasonable excuse. You might be successful with your appeal if there is clear evidence that your cheque was lost in the post or in the event of serious illness. Lack of funds, apart from exceptional circumstances, or cheques wrongly made out are examples of cases when your appeal would be rejected.

The Inland Revenue booklet SA/BK5 contains examples of what the Inland Revenue will regard as a reasonable excuse for appealing against a surcharge for the late payment of tax.

Penalties

The main penalties under Self-Assessment are:

Offence	Penalty
You do not submit your Tax Return to your Tax Office by 31 January after the end of the tax year	£100
Your Return is still outstanding after a further 6 months	Further £100

The above penalties are automatic but will be reduced if the tax owing is less. Up to £60 per day in further penalties can be levied on application to the Commissioners by the Inland Revenue.

Returns still outstanding after the anniversary of the filing date	£200 and a further sum up to the amount of the tax payable
You don't receive a Tax Return and fail to notify the Inland Revenue of chargability to tax within 6 months of the end of the tax year	Not exceeding the tax due
Fraudulently or negligently delivering an incorrect Tax Return	Up to the amount of the difference between the tax actually payable and that which was shown as due
Failure to produce documents during an Inland Revenue enquiry	An initial penalty of £50 followed by a further penalty of up to £30 for each day during which the failure continues
Failure to maintain and keep records	Up to £3,000
Fraudulently or negligently claiming to reduce interim tax payments	Up to an amount equivalent to the difference between the tax paid and the tax that should have been paid

Generally a penalty determination must be made, or proceedings commenced, within 6 years of the date on which the penalty was incurred.

The rules allow for this to be extended to any later time within 3 years of the final determination of the tax liability.

In February 1998 the Inland Revenue issued a Press Release outlining the limited circumstances, for the first year of Self-Assessment, when taxpayers will be let off the £100 late filing penalty. The announcement reads:

'Where taxpayers have filed their Returns but made an oversight – such as forgetting to sign their forms or not including one or two pieces of information – they will have had their forms returned to them and could face a penalty. The Inland Revenue will use their discretion so that, where forms which were already returned to taxpayers are corrected and sent back to the Inland Revenue by 11 February, they will be regarded as having met the deadline. If similar oversights are spotted in the next few weeks a similar discretion will be exercised.'

Furthermore, if taxpayers have a genuinely good excuse for missing the deadline, they can appeal against the penalty.

Examples of what may be accepted by the Inland Revenue as a reasonable excuse include:

- Where the Tax Return was not received by the taxpayer.

- Where the Tax Return was lost in the post or delayed because of:

    — fire or flood at the Post Office where the Tax Return was handled.

    — prolonged industrial action within the Post Office.

    — an unforeseen event which disrupted the postal services.

- Where a taxpayer lost his or her tax records as a result of fire, flood or theft.

- Serious illness.

- Death of a spouse, domestic partner or close relative.

Examples of what the Inland Revenue will not agree as a reasonable excuse include:

- Tax Return too difficult.

- Pressure of work.

- Lack of information.

- Absence of reminders from the Inland Revenue.

16

ELECTIONS AND CLAIMS – TIME LIMITS

You will already have gathered that certain options available to you as a taxpayer are dependent on you submitting an election or claim to the appropriate authority. As these will usually involve a saving in tax it is important to appreciate that you often need to act within prescribed time limits. This chapter brings together those elections and claims which are most likely to concern you. It also sets out the time available during which they must be submitted to the Inspector of Taxes or Customs and Excise. It is by no means exhaustive.

Election/Claim	Time Limit
Chapter 3 – Personal Allowances and Reliefs	
By a wife to receive one half of the married couple's allowance	Before the start of the tax year for which it is to have effect
An election for the married couple's allowance to be deducted wholly from a wife's total income	As above
A subsequent election by a husband to take back one half of the married couple's allowance	As above
Withdrawal of any of the above elections	As above
Claim to the various personal allowances detailed in the chapter	No later than five years after 31 January next following the end of the tax year
Transfer of excess allowances between husband and wife	No later than five years after 31 January next following the end of the tax year
Chapter 4 – Interest Payments and Other Outgoings	
Election for mortgage interest payable by one spouse to be treated as if payable by the other spouse, or revocation of such an election	Within 12 months after 31 January following the end of the tax year

Opting out of the MIRAS scheme where part of your home is let	Within 22 months of the end of the tax year in which you want the new arrangement to begin

Chapter 6 – Value Added Tax

Application for Registration	No later than 30 days from the end of the month after the one when turnover exceeds the registration limit
Submission to Customs and Excise of each VAT Return with full payment of the tax due	Within one month after the end of the VAT accounting period
Claim for Bad Debt Relief	When a debt remains unpaid for more than six months

Chapter 7 – The Self-Employed

Relief for post-cessation expenses	No later than one year after 31 January next following the tax year in which the payments are made
Creating a separate pool to work out the capital allowances on an asset with a short life expectancy	No later than one year after 31 January next following the tax year in which the period of account ended in which the expenditure is incurred
Notification of a claim to capital allowances on expenditure on plant and machinery	
Relief for the loss sustained in the tax year against other income of the same year or the preceding year	Within one year after 31 January next following the tax year in which the loss arose
Relief for a trading loss against the profits arising from the same trade in subsequent periods	Within five years after the 31 January next following the tax year in which the loss was sustained
Relief for the loss in the first four years of assessment of a new business to be given against the income of the three preceding years of assessment	No later than one year after 31 January next following the tax year in which the loss occurred
Relief for trading losses to be offset against Capital Gains	No later than one year after the 31 January next following the tax year

Relief for the loss in the last 12 months of trading to be given against the profits of the same trade which were assessed in the three tax years prior to the year in which the trade was discontinued	Within five years after the 31 January next following the tax year in which the trade ceased

Chapter 9 – Personal Pensions

Personal pension premiums to be treated as paid in the preceding year of assessment	By 31 January after the tax year in which payment was made
Retirement annuity premiums to be treated as paid in the preceding year of assessment	By 31 January after the tax year in which payment was made

Chapter 10 – Investment Income

An election to opt out of the Rent-a-Room relief for a particular tax year, or withdrawl of an election	Within one year after 31 January next following the tax year
An election for the alternative basis of Rent-a-Room relief, or revocation of an election	Within one year after 31 January next following the tax year
Claim for relief under the Enterprise Investment Scheme	Within five years after 31 January next following that in which the shares were issued
Declaration by a married couple that their beneficial interest in joint property and the income arising from it are unequal	The date of the declaration

Chapter 11 – The Family Unit

An election for the income tax treatment of maintenance payments under obligations which existed on 15 March 1988 to change to the basis appropriate to arrangements made since then	By the payer within one year after 31 January next following the first tax year for which it is to apply. The election cannot be revoked

Chapter 13 – Capital Gains Tax

Claims to the capital loss where the value of an asset becomes negligible	The loss arises on the date of claim although, in practice, a two-year period is allowed from the end of the tax year in which the asset became of negligible value
Claim for the loss on shares that were originally subscribed for in an unquoted trading company to be set against income in the year of loss, or the preceding year	No later than one year after 31 January next following the tax year in which the loss was made
An election for the capital gains on disposals of assets you owned on 31 March 1982 to be worked out by reference to their values on that date, ignoring original costs	Within one year after 31 January next following the tax year in which the first disposal of an asset you owned on 31 March 1982 takes place
Claim for the 6 April 1965 value to be substituted in a calculation of the capital gain arising on the sale of an asset held at that date	No later than one year after 31 January next following the tax year in which the disposal is made
An election to determine which of your homes is to be regarded as your principal residence for Capital Gains Tax purposes	Two years from the date when two or more properties are eligible
Claim to reinvestment relief on the disposal of assets giving rise to chargeable gains	Within five years after the 31 January next following the tax year to which it relates
Claim to roll-over relief on the disposal of business assets	No later than five years after 31 January next following the tax year to which it relates
Claim to a reduction in the deferred gain on assets acquired in the period 31 March 1982 to 5 April 1988	Within one year after 31 January next following the tax year in which the disposal takes place

The time limits for elections and claims for both Income Tax and Capital Gains Tax have been amended since Self-Assessment came into effect for 1996/97 onwards.

17

INHERITANCE TAX

Inheritance Tax was introduced in 1986 as the successor to Capital Transfer Tax. Not only might Inheritance Tax be payable on transfers or gifts you make during your lifetime, but it is also due on the value of your estate on death. Husband and wife are treated as separate individuals, and both are entitled to the various exemptions. Inheritance Tax is far from straightforward. What follows is a brief outline. The Tax is administered by the Capital Taxes Office, to whom any Returns should be submitted.

Potentially exempt transfers

The most significant feature of Inheritance Tax is the concept of a potentially exempt transfer (PET). This is:

- an outright gift to an individual;

- a gift into an accumulation-and-maintenance settlement;

- a gift into a settlement for the benefit of a disabled person;

- a gift into an interest in possession trust;

- the termination of an interest in possession settlement where the settled property passes to an individual, an accumulation-and-maintenance settlement, or a trust for the benefit of a disabled person.

No tax is payable providing the donor lives for at least seven years after making the gift. A form of tapering relief applies where death occurs within seven years. The amount of Inheritance Tax is then calculated at the rates which apply at the date of death as shown in the following table:

Number of Years between Gift and Death	% of Tax Payable
Not more than 3	100
Between 3 and 4	80
Between 4 and 5	60
Between 5 and 6	40
Between 6 and 7	20

Suppose, however, the PET is within the limit of chargeable transfers taxable at a nil rate. There will then be no benefit from tapering relief as no Inheritance Tax is payable on the PET.

Gifts with reservation

If you make a gift but continue to enjoy some benefit from it, the property or asset you have given away is likely to be treated as yours until either the date when you cease to enjoy any benefit from the gift, or your death. This is a 'gift with reservation'. For example, you give your house to your children but continue to live there, rent free. Your house would then be counted as part of your estate and the seven year period would not start until you either moved home or began to pay a commercial rent.

Lifetime gifts

If you make a gift during your lifetime which is not a potentially exempt transfer it will attract liability to Inheritance Tax at one half of the rates which apply on death. An example of such a lifetime gift is a transfer into a discretionary trust.

Exemptions

The main exemptions applicable to individuals are:

- transfers between husband and wife, during lifetime and on death;

- gifts up to £3,000 in any one tax year. Any part of the exemption which is left over can be carried forward to the following year only. For example, if your total transfers came to £1,500 during 1996/97 you could have given away as much as £4,500 during 1997/98 all within your annual exemption limit. However, if your gifts totalled £3,000 in 1996/97, you would be limited to £3,000 in 1997/98 as well;

- gifts to any one person up to £250 per person in each tax year. Where the total amount given to any one individual exceeds this limit no part comes within this exemption;

- marriage gifts. The amount you can give away in consideration of marriage depends on your relationship to the bride or groom, as follows:

	£
By either parent	5,000
By a grandparent or great-grandparent	2,500
By any other person	1,000

- regular gifts out of income which form part of your normal expenditure;

- gifts to charities and 'qualifying' political parties, both without limit. Both these exceptions apply to lifetime gifts and to bequests on death;

- lump sums paid out of your Pension Scheme on death. The trustees should have discretion over who receives the cash payments.

Business property

Subject to certain conditions, qualifying business assets and interests in businesses qualify for relief for transfers arising either in lifetime or on death. There are two rates:

100% for:

- unincorporated businesses;

- all holdings of unquoted shares in qualifying companies.

50% for:

- shares giving control of a quoted company;

- land, buildings, machinery or plant used in a partnership or controlled company where the transferor is a partner or controlling shareholder.

Unquoted shares include those traded on the Unlisted Securities Market (USM) and the Alternative Investment Market (AIM).

Agricultural property

The reliefs applying to agricultural land and holdings are similar to those for business property. Subject to certain minimum ownership and use conditions, the two rates are again:

100% for:

- land and buildings where the transferor has vacant possession, or the right to obtain it, within 12 months;

- agricultural property let for periods exceeding 12 months where the letting commenced on or after 1 September 1995.

50% for:

- other qualifying property.

Trusts

There are special provisions covering the application of Inheritance Tax to different types of Trust. Perhaps the three most common forms of trust are:

- Interest in Possession Trusts where someone is entitled to the trust income as and when it arises. For Inheritance Tax purposes the person so entitled is deemed to own the trust assets personally;

- Discretionary Trusts, where income is distributed at the discretion of the trustees. There are complex rules for computing the liabilities which can arise when assets pass from the trust to beneficiaries.

A further charge arises on the assets in the trust on each tenth anniversary from its commencement;

- Accumulation and Maintenance Trusts, which, generally, provide for young members of a family. To qualify under this category the trust must provide that someone will become entitled to either the capital or the income of the trust by the age of 25. Until then no interest in possession must exist. For such qualifying trusts, no charge to Inheritance Tax arises when the beneficiaries become entitled.

Rates of tax

Each taxable gift or transfer is not considered in isolation in calculating how much tax is payable on it. In working out how much is payable, previous taxable transfers are taken into account. This is because the tax due on each chargeable gift or the value of your estate on death is dependent upon the cumulative value of all other chargeable transfers in the seven years leading up to the date of the next chargeable transfer. The rates payable on death from 6 April 1997 are:

Band	Rate
£	%
0-215,000	0
Over 215,000	40

These rates also apply to all lifetime gifts or transfers within three years of death. Inheritance Tax payable on PETS more than three years before but within seven years of death is determined by the first table in this chapter.

The limit of £200,000 on chargeable transfers taxable at a nil rate is increased each year in the same way as the main personal Income Tax allowances.

Illustration

Wendy Brown, a widow, died on 30 September 1997 leaving her entire estate to her daughter. She did not make any gifts in the seven years leading up to her death. Her assets and unpaid bills on her death were:

Assets	Value	
	£	£
Flat	160,000	
Household effects	2,000	
Car	5,000	
Building society account	30,000	
Shares	40,000	
Current account	2,500	
		239,500

Less: Allowable Deductions

Funeral expenses	920	
Income Tax	500	
Telephone bill	50	
Electricity bill	60	
	————	1,530

Net Value of Estate	£237,970

Inheritance Tax Payable

On first £215,000	Nil
On next £22,970 at 40%	£9,188
	£9,188

The tax is payable out of Wendy Brown's estate by the executors of her will.

Sales at a loss

Relief is available where certain assets are sold during specified periods after death for less than the valuation at the date of death. In the case of land and buildings, the period is four years. For quoted securities the time limit is one year. The relief is available to 'the appropriate person' (the one who pays the tax). All sales by that person in the respective periods must be aggregated. As a result, losses may accordingly be reduced or eliminated by profits so that the relief could be restricted or lost. When this type of relief is due, the net proceeds of sale are substituted for the valuation at death. The Inheritance Tax liability is then recalculated.

Payment of tax

The persons primarily liable for payment of Inheritance Tax are:

- the transferor in respect of chargeable lifetime gifts;

- the personal representatives on death.

  The due dates for payment are:

- for chargeable lifetime gifts – 6 months after the end of the month in which the gift was made;

- for potentially exempt transfers which become chargeable on death, and the charge on death itself – 6 months after the end of the month in which the death occurred.

There is an option to pay the tax on certain types of assets by ten equal annual instalments. The first payment is due on the normal due date.

The relevant assets are:

- land and buildings;

- controlling shareholdings;

- unquoted shares, subject to certain conditions;

- businesses.

In the case of lifetime transfers which are, or become, chargeable, the instalment option is only available if the tax is borne by the transferee. Where the asset is sold during the instalment paying period, outstanding instalments become payable immediately.

Interest is payable on Inheritance Tax liabilities from the due date until the date of payment. At the time of going to print the rate of interest is 5%. Where the instalment option is in force, no interest is payable on the outstanding instalments except on:

- land and buildings which do not qualify for business property or agricultural property relief;

- shares and securities in investment companies.

Legacies

Any Inheritance Tax due on a legacy you receive under a will will be accounted for by the executors of the estate before the legacy is paid over to you. You do not pay either Income Tax or Capital Gains Tax on a legacy. It does not need to be reported on your annual Tax Return.

Intestacy

If you die without having made a will your estate will be divided up under the statutory intestacy rules. If you are married and survived by both your spouse and children, your spouse is entitled to a statutory legacy of £125,000. This increases to £200,000 if there are no children but you are survived by specific relatives.

The present intestacy rules for individuals who die domiciled in England or Wales can best be summarized as follows:

Unmarried Individual

Survived by	Division of Estate
(1) Children	Divided equally between them
(2) No children but parents	Shared equally between them
(3) Neither children nor parents, but brothers and sisters	Divided equally between them
(4) No children, parents, brothers, sisters but grandparents	Shared equally between them
(5) Only aunts and uncles	Divided equally between them
(6) No relatives as listed above	Estate passes to Crown

Married Individual

Particular Circumstances	Division
(1) Estate amounts to less than £125,000	All to spouse
(2) Estate exceeds £125,000 and there are children	Spouse is entitled to first £125,000 and a life interest in half the remainder. The balance is divided between the children
(3) Estate is worth less than £200,000 and there are no children	All to spouse
(4) Estate comes to more than £200,000, the couple have no children but parents are still alive	Spouse receives first £200,000 and half the remainder absolutely. The parents share the rest
(5) As in (4) above, parents are dead, but there are brothers and sisters	As in (4) above but the balance is shared between the brothers and sisters instead of the parents
(6) The only survivor is the spouse	All to spouse

The spouse must survive the intestate individual by 28 days to become entitled under the intestacy rules.

In Scotland the intestacy rules have no application to estates of individuals who die domiciled there. Furthermore, a surviving spouse and/or children are entitled to fixed proportions of the moveable estate of the deceased individual. This rule applies whether the deceased died intestate or had made a will.

18

TAX SAVING HINTS

Saving tax is not always so straight forward as it sounds. To make a meaningful reduction in your annual tax bill will usually necessitate reorganising your finances and investments. As a general rule opportunities to save tax should not be considered without due regard to other criteria.

First and foremost comes your own personal circumstances. If you are a married man, maybe your wife has a low taxable income? You know that if you transfer some investments into her own name she will then benefit from her full personal allowance. Between you, your annual tax bill is reduced, perhaps significantly. But remember that the investments given to your wife will then belong to her. Most couples will continue to enjoy the benefits from their saving in tax for many years to come. This is not so for everyone – some couples will split up. While no couple ever wants to contemplate that their marriage might break down, the prospect of this happening should, at the very least, be borne in mind in any tax-planning exercise involving a transfer of assets between spouses. The same rule applies if you are thinking about making gifts to your children. They have been known to squander money and subsequently fall out with their parents.

When it comes to investments, remember that you will sometimes need to be locked into an investment for a number of years to benefit from all the tax attractions that go with it. A typical example of this type of investment is a subscription for new shares in a Venture Capital Trust. Examine the merits of any investment from all angles. Sometimes it will be best to steer clear of investments which are inflexible. You could end up endangering your family's financial security. The same applies to those investments which carry a higher degree of risk.

In the fast moving world in which we live you must keep your finances under constant review. Although tax rates have been substantially unchanged for a number of years you may need to adjust your finances to take account of future reductions or increases in the various taxes. You should also be ready to respond to any shift in taxation policy following the change of Government. When it comes to Inheritance Tax, remember it will be the law at some time in the future when you die which will determine the tax payable by your executors.

Self-Assessment

- Remember the two important dates for sending back your complete and signed Tax Return. These are 30 September and 31 January after the end of the tax year. You must send your return back by 30 September if you want the Inland Revenue to calculate your tax. If you pay tax under PAYE, and want any underpayment of tax collected by an adjustment to your PAYE code number in the following year, you must also submit your Return by 30 September.

- Do not forget that the second send-back date of 31 January is critical. You must stick to it. Otherwise a fixed penalty will automatically be applied.

- Always pay your tax on time. If you are late in making payment then not only will you be charged interest but you also run the risk of incurring a surcharge.

- Keep proper records. You will find it easier to complete your Tax Return fully and accurately. Furthermore, if your tax office decides to enquire into your Tax Return the records you have kept will help you demonstrate that your Return is accurate and complete in all respects. Remember also to keep your records for the right length of time.

- Around each January/February look out for your new PAYE coding notice for the following tax year. Make sure you have been given the right allowances and that any deductions for unpaid tax or benefits-in-kind are correct. Get in touch with your Tax Office if anything is unclear.

Allowances and reliefs

- Every taxpayer, man or woman, single or married, is entitled to the personal allowance. Married couples should consider transferring their income-producing assets between them to maximize personal allowances and, where possible, the lower and/or basic rate tax bands.

- Married couples should not forget to consider whether the rules governing the transfer of the married couple's allowance between husband and wife can save them tax.

- Elderly couples need to pay even more care and attention to their respective incomes. They should make sure they do not lose out on the higher personal and married couple's age allowances for pensioners in the 65-74 and over 74 age brackets. They should keep an eye on the annual income limit above which allowances are restricted. It may pay them to shift some of their savings income into tax-free investments such as National Savings, TESSAs or PEPs. By doing so, they avoid losing some of their age-related allowances.

- Check on your entitlement to the additional personal allowance if you are single and looking after children.

- If you are recently widowed you are due the special widow's bereavement allowance.

Company car benefits

- If you have the use of a company car keep an eye on your annual business mileage. Maintain a record of your business mileage including the dates and business trips made.

- The car-benefit charge is now 35% of the list price of your car. Where you do between 2,500 and 17,999 miles a year on business it is reduced by one-third. This reduction increases to two-thirds if your business mileage comes to 18,000 or more.

- Plan carefully for the replacement of your company car bearing in mind the reduced car-benefit charge for cars over four years old.

- When the time comes to replace your company car make sure you review your business mileage carefully in the year of change. This is because you may wish to claim the reduced car-benefit charge where you drive more than either 2,500 or 18,000 miles on business. If you fail to accomplish these thresholds pro rata during the year, the Inland Revenue will rule that you have not fulfilled the necessary criteria for the reduced benefit-in-kind.

- You face a further taxable benefit if it is your employer's policy to meet the cost of petrol for private motoring. You will often be better off paying for your own petrol for non-business travel where your private mileage is low.

Value Added Tax

- If your business is not VAT registered, maintain a regular check on your turnover to make sure you are not exceeding the limit for registration.

- Sometimes it pays to apply for voluntary registration. You may be able to reclaim significant amounts of VAT on purchases for and expenses of your business. However, check on your customers to make sure they are VAT registered and will be able to reclaim the VAT charged on your invoices.

- Look into the merits of cash accounting if your annual turnover is less than £350,000.

Sole traders

- Maintain proper books and records for your business. Make sure they are accurate and always up to date. Avoid using estimates.

- Where appropriate pay your wife a proper and fair salary for the secretarial or other assistance she gives you.

- Consider taking your wife into partnership where she helps you in your business and your annual profits are such that the top slice is taxable at the higher 40% rate.

- If you are thinking about buying plant and machinery or, for example, a new car, then it may be better to do so towards the end of your accounting year rather than early in the following year. You benefit from the capital allowances due on the expenditure at an earlier date.

- Explore all the options available for claiming tax relief due on a business loss. You may well find that one or other of the different alternative types of loss-relief claim produces a bigger tax repayment for you. In doing your calculations do not overlook the impact of the tax-free repayment supplement paid by the Inland Revenue.

Pensions

- Put pension savings at the forefront of your personal financial planning.

- Pension schemes offer, perhaps, the greatest scope for tax saving and planning including:

Replacing your income when you retire

Tax relief on premiums at your top rate of tax

No UK tax payable by pension funds

Tax-free lump sum on retirement

Tax-deductible death benefits for your family

Death benefits free of Inheritance Tax

- If you are in employment, look into joining your employer's group scheme if there is one. Consider topping up the pension benefits under the scheme by the payment of additional voluntary contributions.

- If you have not been making the maximum contributions into your retirement annuity contract or personal pension do not forget you are allowed to carry forward the unused relief for up to six years.

- Where you are still paying premiums into a retirement annuity taken out before the beginning of July 1988 it may be better to continue with this policy rather than start a personal pension plan. Do, however, bear in mind the higher annual contribution limits into a personal pension compared with a retirement annuity.

Tax-favoured investments

- Take a look at the investments available from the Department of National Savings where the return is free of both Income Tax and Capital Gains Tax.

- Do not ignore TESSAs. Essentially they are savings accounts, usually with a Bank or Building Society, where the interest is tax free providing the account is held for five years. Do not be deterred by the five year savings term. You can usually get access to your savings at an earlier date – all you lose is the tax benefit on the interest.

- A PEP is an investment in shares, an Investment Trust or Unit Trust where the dividends and interest are free of Income Tax. Profits in a PEP are not subject to Capital Gains Tax. You do not have to declare your PEP investments on your Tax Return.

- Venture Capital Trusts are tax-efficient vehicles aimed at encouraging investment in unquoted companies in the UK. Bear in mind, therefore, that an investment in a Venture Capital Trust carries a higher degree of risk. The tax benefits for a *'qualifying subscriber'* are:

  20% Income Tax relief on the amount invested
  Deferral of Capital Gains Tax on gains re-invested
  Tax-free income and capital gains

- Investments under the Enterprise Investment Scheme are also high risk with tax benefits not dissimilar to Venture Capital Trust investments.

Capital Gains

- Wherever possible try and utilise fully your annual Capital Gains Tax exemption limit. Any part of the limit not used cannot be carried forward to future years.

- Husband and wife each have their own annual exemption limit. They should plan to make maximum use of both exemptions.

- The well-known practice of *'Bed and Breakfasting'* shares under the simple procedure of sale and repurchase on consecutive days in the same Stock Exchange Account is one way of realising gains to mop up your annual exemption limit. The same method can also be used to establish losses and reduce your net taxable gains in a tax year below the annual exemption limit.

- Do not forget that the excess of your chargeable gains over and above the exemption limit is charged at the tax rates found by adding the excess to your taxable income. By realising losses you may be able to substantially reduce your Capital Gains Tax liability – particularly if you are a 40% taxpayer.

- Are you running your own business and thinking about retiring early? The exemption from tax on retirement of the first £250,000, and 50% of the next £750,000, of capital gains on business assets is a most valuable relief. However, the qualifying conditions are complicated.

For maximum relief you must meet them for 10 years before you sell up and do nothing in the following 10 years that risks losing the relief.

- Perhaps you have sold some assets and face a substantial Capital Gains Tax bill on the profits realized? Then why not consider Reinvestment Relief. Only the gain, not the sale proceeds, have to be reinvested.

- If you have two homes, you are allowed to make an election stipulating which of your homes you want to be regarded as your principal private residence for Capital Gains Tax purposes. The profit on a sale of this home will be exempt from tax. Remember that the election must be made within two years from the date when two or more properties are eligible.

- Where it is to your advantage, do not overlook making an election for the gains and losses on disposals of assets which you owned on 31 March 1982 to be calculated solely by reference to their market value at that date. The time limit for making the election is two years after the end of the tax year in which the first disposal of an asset you owned on 31 March 1982 takes place.

Miscellaneous

- As a first time buyer, or whenever you move home, have regard to the overall £30,000 loan limit for mortgage interest tax relief. Remember it applies to any one home rather than to each borrower. Unmarried couples jointly buying a home have to share the maximum limit between them.

- If you can, make your charitable donations under Deed of Covenant or the Gift Aid Scheme. Charities can then claim repayment of the tax you deduct at the basic rate. If you are liable to tax at the top rate of 40% you will also profit as you can deduct such payments in working out your annual higher-rate tax liability.

- Non-taxpayers should get the special form so they can receive their Bank and Building Society interest gross, that is with no deduction for tax. Non-taxpayers are most likely to be pensioners, children or dependent married women.

- If you are letting furnished accommodation in your home, consider whether you can benefit from Rent-a-Room relief. Gross annual rents below £4,250 are tax free.

- Foreign nationals living in the UK should make the most of their non-UK domicile status for tax purposes. Such individuals are not subject to UK taxation on either overseas investment income or capital gains unless the investment income or capital gains are remitted to, or enjoyed in, the UK.

- Remember that if you are working abroad and you can establish a consecutive period of at least 365 days overseas the exemption from Income Tax on your earnings from this employment is 100%. Intermittent visits to the UK are allowed in establishing a qualifying period of at least 365 days. Be warned, however, that these must not amount to more than 62 days, nor in building up the qualifying period must they come to more than ⅙th of the period starting from the outset.

- Grandparents, or other relatives with the means, can fund tax efficiently for school fees and other costs of educating and maintaining children. This is best done via a Trust. The income the Trustees pay out counts as the children's income for tax purposes. They should be able to reclaim all or part of the tax suffered by the Trustees by off-setting it against their personal allowance.

Inheritance Tax

- Remember that gifts and transfers between husbands and wives are exempt from Inheritance Tax.

- Whenever you can afford to do so, make use of the various exemptions detailed in Chapter 17.

- The 'normal expenditure out of income' exemption is ideal for paying premiums on life policies written in Trust for the next generations. The policy proceeds will pass to them free of tax.

- While both gifts and legacies to charities are exempt for Inheritance Tax purposes, a lifetime gift to a charity can have attractive Income Tax benefits, both for the charity and the donor, which do not apply to legacies.

- Gifts outside the exemptions should be made as early as possible to increase your chances of surviving the seven year period. Make immediately chargeable gifts – for example to Discretionary Settlements – before potentially exempt transfers.

- Give assets that do not qualify for relief before those that do.

- Consider restricting chargeable legacies for the next generations to the nil rate band, leaving the rest of your estate to your spouse. He or she can then make gifts and hopefully survive a further seven years.

- Do not waste your nil rate band. Even if you want to leave everything to your spouse, ask about Discretionary Wills. The potential saving in tax for the next generations is significant.

- Where possible look into rearranging your affairs to take advantage of the business or agricultural property reliefs.

- In the two years after death, consider the use of a Deed of Variation in order to utilize any available exemptions which would otherwise be lost.

TABLE 1

<small>INLAND REVENUE EXPLANATORY BOOKLETS</small>

No.	Title
IR 1	Extra Statutory Concessions
IR 14/15	Construction Industry Tax Deduction Scheme
IR 17	Share Acquisitions by Directors and Employees: An outline for Employees
IR 20	Residents and Non-Residents – Liability to Tax in the United Kingdom
IR 24	Class 4 National Insurance Contributions
IR 28	Starting in Business
IR 33	Income Tax and School Leavers
IR 34	Pay As You Earn
IR 37	Appeals against Tax
IR 40	Conditions for getting a Sub-Contractor's Tax Certificate
IR 41	Income Tax and the Unemployed
IR 42	Lay-Offs and Short-Time Working
IR 43	Income Tax and Strikes
IR 45	What to do about Tax when Someone Dies
IR 53	Thinking of Taking Someone On? PAYE for Employers
IR 56	Employed or Self-Employed? A Guide for Tax and National Insurance
IR 57	Thinking of Working for Yourself?
IR 58	Going to Work Abroad?
IR 60	Income Tax and Students
IR 64	Giving to Charity: How Businesses can get Tax Relief
IR 65	Giving to Charity: How Individuals can get Tax Relief
IR 68	Income Tax – Accrued Income Scheme
IR 69	Expenses Payments: Forms P11D – How to Save Yourself Work
IR 71	PAYE Inspection: Employers' and Contractors' Records
IR 72	Investigations: The Examination of Business Accounts
IR 73	Inland Revenue Investigations: How Settlements are Negotiated
IR 78	Personal Pensions: A Guide for Tax
IR 80	Income Tax and Married Couples
IR 87	Letting and your Home
IR 89	Personal Equity Plans: A Guide for Potential Investors
IR 90	Tax Allowances and Reliefs
IR 91	A Guide for Widows and Widowers
IR 92	A Guide for One-Parent Families
IR 93	Separation, Divorce and Maintenance Payments
IR 95	Approved Profit-Sharing Schemes – An Outline for Employees
IR 97	Approved SAYE Share Option Schemes – An Outline for Employees Schemes

IR 101   Approved Company Share Option Plans – An Outline for
          Employees
IR 103   Tax Relief for Private Medical Insurance
IR 104   Simple Tax Accounts
IR 105   How your Profits are Taxed
IR 109   PAYE Inspections and Negotiations: Employers' and Contractors'
          Records: How Settlements are Negotiated
IR 110   A Guide for People with Savings
IR 113   Gift Aid: A Guide for Donors and Charities
IR 114   TESSA: Tax-free interest for Taxpayers
IR 115   Tax and Childcare
IR 116   Guide for Sub-Contractors with Tax Certificates
IR 117   A Sub-Contractor's Guide to the Deduction Scheme
IR 119   Tax Relief for Vocational Training
IR 120   You and the Inland Revenue (General)
IR 121   Income Tax and Pensioners
IR 122   Volunteer Drivers
IR 123   Mortgage Interest Relief – Buying Your Home
IR 125   Using Your Own Car for Work
IR 127   Are You Paying Too Much Tax on Your Savings?
IR 131   Statements of Practice
IR 133   Income Tax and Company Cars: A Guide for Employees
IR 134   Income Tax and Relocation Packages
IR 136   Income Tax and Company Vans: A Guide for Employees
          and Employers
IR 137   The Enterprise Investment Scheme
IR 138   Living or Retiring Abroad?
IR 139   Income from Abroad?
IR 140   Non-Resident Landlords, their Agents and Tenants
IR 141   Open Government
IR 144   Income Tax and Incapacity Benefit
IR 145   Low Interest Loans Provided by Employers: A Guide for
          Employees
IR 148   Are Your Workers Employed or Self-Employed? A Guide to
          Tax and National Insurance for Contractors in the
          Construction Industry
IR 150   Taxation of Rents – A Guide to Property Income
IR 152   Trusts: An Introduction
IR 153   Tax Exemption for Sickness or Unemployment Insurance Payments
IR 155   PAYE: Settlement Agreements
IR 157   Workers in Building and Construction – Help with Tax for
          Employees and the Self-Employed
IR 160   Enquiries under Self-Assessment
SA/BK3   Self-Assessment – A Guide to Keeping Records for the
          Self-Employed

SA/BK4   Self-Assessment – A General Guide to Keeping Records
SA/BK6   Self-Assessment – Penalties for Late Tax Returns
SA/BK7   Self-Assessment – Surcharges for Late Payment of Tax
SA/BK8   Self-Assessment – Your Guide
480   Expenses and Benefits: A Guide for Tax
P7/P8   Employers' Guides to PAYE
CGT 4   Capital Gains Tax: Owner-Occupied Houses
CGT 6   Retirement Relief on Disposal of a Business
CGT 11   Capital Gains Tax and Small Businesses
CGT 14   Capital Gains Tax: An Introduction
CGT 16   Capital Gains Tax: Indexation Allowance –
         Disposals after 5 April 1988
IHT 2   Inheritance Tax on Lifetime Gifts
IHT 3   An Introduction to Inheritance Tax
IHT 8   Alterations to an Inheritance following a Death
IHT 14   Inheritance Tax – The Personal Representatives Responsibilities
IHT 15   Inheritance Tax – How to Calculate the Liability
IHT 16   Inheritance Tax – Settled Property
IHT 17   Inheritance Tax – Business, Farms and Woodlands
IHT 18   Inheritance Tax – Foreign Aspects

TABLE 2

FLAT-RATE ALLOWANCES FOR SPECIAL CLOTHING
AND THE UPKEEP OF TOOLS – 1997/98

(1) Fixed rate for all occupations

	£
Agricultural	70
Forestry	70
Quarrying	70
Brass and copper	100
Precious metals	70
Textile prints	60
Food	40
Glass	60
Railways	70
Uniformed prison officers	55
Uniformed bank employees	40
Uniformed police officers up to and including chief inspector	55

(2) Variable rate depending on category of occupation

Seamen	130/135
Iron mining	75/100
Iron and steel	45/60/120
Aluminium	45/60/100/130
Engineering	45/60/100/120
Shipyards	45/60/75/115
Vehicles	40/60/105
Particular engineering	45/60/100/120
Constructional engineering	45/60/75/115
Electrical and electricity supply	25/90
Textiles	60/85
Clothing	30/45
Leather	40/55
Printing	30/70/105
Building materials	40/55/85
Wood and furniture	45/75/90/115
Building	40/55/85/105
Heating	70/90/100
Public service	40/55

Note

The allowances are only available to manual workers who have to bear the cost of upkeep of tools and special clothing. Other employees, such as office staff, cannot claim them.

TABLE 3

VAT NOTICES AND LEAFLETS

No.	Title
999	Catalogue of Publications
700	The VAT Guide
700/1	Should I be Registered for VAT?
700/11	Cancelling your Registration
700/12	Filling in your VAT Return
700/15	The Ins and Outs of VAT
700/21	Keeping Records and Accounts
700/41	Late Registration: Penalty
700/42	Misdeclaration Penalty
700/43	Default Interest
700/45	How to Correct Errors you find on your VAT Returns
700/50	Default Surcharge Appeals
700/51	VAT Enquiries Guide
700/54	What If I don't Pay?
725	The Single Market
727	Retail Schemes
731	Cash Accounting
732	Annual Accounting
748	Extra Statutory Concessions
989	Visits by Customs and Excise Officers

TABLE 4

BUSINESS ECONOMIC NOTES

BEN	1	Travel Agents
BEN	2	Road Haulage
BEN	3	Lodging Industry
BEN	4	Hairdressers
BEN	5	Waste Materials, Reclamation and Disposal
BEN	6	Funeral Directors
BEN	7	Dentists
BEN	8	Florists
BEN	9	Licensed Victuallers
BEN	10	Jewellery Trade
BEN	11	Electrical Retailers
BEN	12	Antique and Fine Art Dealers
BEN	13	Fish and Chip Shops
BEN	14	The Pet Industry
BEN	15	Veterinary Surgeons
BEN	16	Catering – General
BEN	17	Catering – Restaurants
BEN	18	Catering – Fast Foods, Cafés and Snack Bars
BEN	19	Farming – Stock Valuation for Income Tax purposes
BEN	20	Insurance Brokers and Agents
BEN	21	Residential Rest and Nursing Homes
BEN	22	Dispensing Chemists
BEN	23	Driving Instructors
BEN	24	Independent Fishmongers
BEN	25	Taxicabs and Private Hire Vehicles
BEN	26	Confectioners, Tobacconists and Newsagents

TABLE 5

RATES OF NATIONAL INSURANCE CONTRIBUTIONS FOR 1997/98

CLASS 1 Contributions for Employees

		Standard Rate		Contracted Out	
		On First £62.00	On Remainder	On First £62.00	On Remainder
Contributions levied on all weekly earnings if they reach	£62.00				
but do not exceed	£465.00	2%	10%	2%	8.2%
If weekly earnings exceed	£465.00	No Additional Contributions		No Additional Contributions	

Reduced Rate for Married Women and Widows with a Valid Election Certificate	3.85%
	£
Men over 65 and Women over 60	Nil
Lower Earnings Limit — Weekly	62.00
— Monthly	269.00
— Annually	3,224.00
Upper Earnings Limit — Weekly	465.00
— Monthly	2,015.00
— Annually	24,180.00

CLASS 2 Contributions for the Self-Employed

Weekly flat rate	6.15
Small earnings exception	3,480.00

CLASS 3 Voluntary Contributions

Weekly rate	6.05

CLASS 4 Contributions for the Self-Employed
6% of profits
between £7,010
and £24,180

TABLE 6

DSS EXPLANATORY PAMPHLETS

CA01	National Insurance for Employees
CA02	National Insurance for Self-Employed People with Small Earnings
CA03	National Insurance Contributions for Self-Employed People
CA04	Class 2 and Class 3 National Insurance Contributions: Direct Debit – The Easy Way to Pay
CA06	Working for Yourself
CA07	National Insurance: Unpaid and Late-Paid Contributions
CA08	National Insurance Voluntary Contributions
CA09	National Insurance for Widows
CA10	National Insurance for Divorced Women
CA12	Training for Further Employment and Your NI Record
CA13	National Insurance Choices for Married Women
CA17	Employees' Guide to Minimum Contributions
CA44	National Insurance for Company Directors
CA46	Useful Contacts and Leaflets for Employers
NI196	Social Security Benefit Rates

TABLE 7

SOCIAL SECURITY BENEFITS

Taxable
Incapacity Benefit after the first 28 weeks
Income Support (1)
Industrial Death Benefit Pensions
Invalid Care Allowance (2)
Jobseeker's Allowance
Retirement Pension (2)
Statutory Maternity Pay
Statutory Sick Pay
Widowed Mother's Allowance (2)
Widow's Pension

Non-taxable
Incapacity Benefit for the first 28 weeks of sickness
Income Support (1)
Maternity Allowance
Child Benefit
Child Dependency Additions to Benefits
Child's Special Allowance
Christmas Bonus for Pensioners
Industrial Injury Benefits
War Disablement Benefits
Disability Living and Working Allowances
Widow's Payment
Family Credit
Guardian's Allowance
Housing Benefit
Jobfinder's Grant
War Widow's, Widower's or Dependent's Pension
Social Fund Payments
Attendance Allowance
Council Tax Benefit
Redundancy Payment
Vaccine Damage (Lump Sum)

Notes
(1) Income Support is only taxable when paid to the unemployed who 'sign on', or to those on strike.
(2) Child dependent additions to these benefits are not taxable.

TABLE 8

MAIN SOCIAL SECURITY BENEFITS FOR 1997/98

	Weekly 7.4.97 Onwards £
Taxable	
Retirement pensions	
Single person	62.45
Married couple's	
both contributors – each	62.45
wife not contributor – addition	37.35
Age addition (over 80) – each	0.25
Widow's benefits	
Widow's pension – standard	62.45
Widowed mother's allowance	62.45
Jobseeker's allowance	
Age 18 to 24	38.90
Age 25 or over	49.15
Incapacity benefit	
Long-term	62.45
Increase for age: higher rate	13.15
lower rate	6.60
Short-term (under pension age) higher rate	55.70
lower rate	47.10
(over pension age) lower and higher rate	59.90
Statutory sick pay	
Standard rate (weekly earnings threshold £62)	55.70
Statutory maternity pay	
Lower rate (weekly earnings threshold £62)	55.70
Non-Taxable	
Maternity allowance	
Higher rate	55.70
Lower rate	48.35
Child benefit	
First child	11.05
Each other child	9.00
Attendance allowance	
Higher rate	49.50
Lower rate	33.10

TABLE 9

Scope of Liability to Income Tax of Earnings

		Duties of employment performed wholly or partly in the UK		Duties of employment performed wholly outside the UK
		In the UK	Outside the UK	
Foreign emoluments [1]	Employee resident and ordinarily resident in the UK	Liable – less possible deduction[2]	Liable – less possible deduction[2]	Liable if received in the UK
	Resident but not ordinarily resident	Liable	Liable if received in the UK	Liable if received in the UK
	Not resident	Liable	Not liable	Not liable
Other earnings	Resident and ordinarily resident	Liable – less possible deduction[2]	Liable – less possible deduction[2]	Liable – less possible deduction[2]
	Resident but not ordinarily resident	Liable	Liable if received in the UK	Liable if received in the UK
	Not resident	Liable	Not liable	Not liable

Notes

(1) 'Foreign emoluments' is the term to mean the earnings of someone who is not domiciled in the UK and whose employer is not resident in, and is resident outside, the UK.

(2) There is a deduction of 100% in these cases from the amount chargeable, if the earnings are for a period which is part of a qualifying absence lasting 365 days or more – this means that such earnings for that period will be free from UK tax.

TABLE 10

CAPITAL GAINS TAX – THE INDEXATION ALLOWANCE

Starting Month for Indexation	Month of Disposal 1997								
	Apr	May	Jun	Jul	Aug	Sept	Oct	Nov	Dec
1982									
Mar	.967	.975	.983	.983	.995	1.005	1.008	1.009	1.014
Apr	.929	.936	.944	.944	.956	.966	.968	.969	.974
May	.915	.922	.930	.930	.942	.952	.954	.955	.960
Jun	.910	.917	.924	.924	.936	.946	.949	.950	.955
Jul	.909	.916	.924	.924	.936	.946	.948	.949	.954
Aug	.908	.916	.923	.923	.935	.945	.947	.949	.954
Sept	.910	.917	.924	.924	.936	.946	.949	.950	.955
Oct	.900	.907	.915	.915	.927	.937	.939	.940	.945
Nov	.891	.898	.905	.905	.917	.927	.930	.931	.936
Dec	.894	.902	.909	.909	.921	.931	.933	.934	.939
1983									
Jan	.892	.899	.907	.907	.919	.928	.931	.932	.937
Feb	.884	.891	.898	.898	.910	.920	.922	.924	.929
Mar	.880	.888	.895	.895	.907	.917	.919	.920	.925
Apr	.854	.862	.869	.869	.881	.890	.892	.894	.898
May	.847	.854	.861	.861	.873	.882	.884	.886	.890
Jun	.842	.849	.856	.856	.868	.878	.880	.881	.886
Jul	.832	.839	.846	.846	.858	.868	.870	.871	.876
Aug	.824	.831	.838	.838	.850	.859	862	.863	.867
Sept	.816	.823	.830	.830	.842	.851	.853	.855	.859
Oct	.810	.817	.824	.824	.835	.845	.847	.848	.853
Nov	.803	.810	.817	.817	.829	.838	.840	.842	.846
Dec	.799	.806	.813	.813	.824	.833	.836	.837	.841
1984									
Jan	.800	.807	.814	.814	.825	.834	.837	.838	.842
Feb	.792	.799	.806	.806	.818	.827	.829	.830	.835
Mar	.787	.794	.800	.800	.812	.821	.823	.824	.829
Apr	.763	.770	.777	.777	.788	.797	.799	.800	.805
May	.757	.763	.770	.770	.781	.790	.793	.794	.798
Jun	.752	.759	.766	.766	.777	.786	.788	.789	.794
Jul	.754	.761	.768	.768	.779	.788	.790	.791	.796
Aug	.738	.745	.751	.751	.762	.771	.773	.775	.779
Sept	.734	.741	.748	.748	.759	.768	.770	.771	.776
Oct	.724	.730	.737	.737	.748	.757	.759	.760	.765
Nov	.719	.725	.732	.732	.743	.752	.754	.755	.759
Dec	.720	.727	.733	.733	.744	.753	.755	.756	.761
1985									
Jan	.714	.720	.727	.727	.738	.747	.749	.750	.754
Feb	.700	.707	.713	.713	.724	.733	.735	.736	.740
Mar	.684	.691	.697	.697	.708	.717	.719	.720	.724
Apr	.649	.655	.662	.662	.672	.681	.683	.684	.688
May	.642	.648	.654	.654	.665	.673	.675	.676	.681

Starting Month for Indexation	Apr	May	Jun	Jul	Month of Disposal 1996 Aug	Sept	Oct	Nov	Dec
Jun	.638	.644	.651	.651	.661	.670	672	.673	.677
Jul	.641	.648	.654	.654	.664	.673	.675	.676	.680
Aug	.637	.643	.649	.649	.660	.668	.670	.671	.676
Sept	.638	.644	.650	.650	.661	.669	.671	.672	.676
Oct	.635	.641	.648	.648	.658	.667	.669	.670	.674
Nov	.630	.636	.642	.642	.652	.661	.663	.664	.668
Dec	.627	.634	.640	.640	.650	.659	.661	.662	.666
1986									
Jan	.624	.630	.636	.636	.647	.655	.657	.658	.662
Feb	.618	.624	.630	.630	.641	.649	.651	.652	.656
Mar	.616	.622	.628	.628	.639	.647	.649	.650	.654
Apr	.600	.606	.613	.613	.623	.631	.633	.634	.638
May	.597	.604	.610	.610	.620	.628	.630	.631	.635
Jun	.598	.604	.611	.611	.621	.629	.631	.632	.636
Jul	.603	.609	.615	.615	.625	.634	.636	.637	.641
Aug	.598	.604	.610	.610	.620	.629	.631	.632	.636
Sept	.590	.596	.602	.602	.612	.621	.623	.624	.628
Oct	.588	.594	.600	.600	.610	.618	.620	.621	.625
Nov	.574	.580	.586	.586	.596	.604	.606	.607	.611
Dec	.569	.575	.581	.581	.591	.599	.601	.602	.606
1987									
Jan	.563	.569	.575	.575	.585	.593	595	.596	.600
Feb	.557	.563	.569	.569	.579	.587	.589	.590	.594
Mar	.554	.560	.566	.566	.576	.583	.585	.586	.590
Apr	.535	.541	.547	.547	.557	.565	.567	.568	.572
May	.534	.540	.546	.546	.555	.563	.565	.566	.570
Jun	.534	.540	.546	.546	.555	.563	.565	.566	.570
Jul	.535	.541	.547	.547	.557	.565	.567	.568	.572
Aug	.531	.537	.543	.543	.552	.560	.562	.563	.567
Sept	.526	.532	.538	.538	.548	.556	.558	.559	.563
Oct	.519	.525	.531	.531	.540	.548	.550	.551	.555
Nov	.512	.517	.523	.523	.533	.541	.543	.544	.547
Dec	.513	.519	.525	.525	.534	.542	.544	.545	.549
1988									
Jan	.513	.519	.525	.525	.534	.542	.544	.545	.549
Feb	.507	.513	.519	.519	.528	.536	.538	.539	.543
Mar	.501	.507	.513	.513	.523	.530	.532	.533	.537
Apr	.477	.483	.489	.489	.498	.506	.508	.509	.512
May	.472	.477	.483	.483	.492	.500	.502	.503	.507
Jun	.466	.472	.477	.477	.487	.494	.496	.497	.501
Jul	.465	.470	.476	.476	.485	.493	.495	.496	.500
Aug	.449	.454	.460	.460	.469	.476	.478	.479	.483
Sept	.442	.447	.453	.453	.462	.470	.471	.472	.476
Oct	.427	.433	.438	.438	.447	.455	.457	.458	.461
Nov	.421	.426	.432	.432	.441	.448	.450	.451	.455
Dec	.417	.422	.428	.428	.437	.444	.446	.447	.451

Starting Month for Indexation				Month of Disposal 1996					
	Apr	May	Jun	Jul	Aug	Sept	Oct	Nov	Dec
1989									
Jan	.408	.414	.419	.419	.428	.435	.437	.438	.441
Feb	.398	.403	.409	.409	.418	.425	.427	.428	.431
Mar	.392	.397	.402	.402	.411	.419	.420	.421	.425
Apr	.367	.373	.378	.378	.387	.394	.395	.396	.400
May	.359	.364	.370	.370	.378	.385	.387	.388	.391
Jun	.354	.360	.365	.365	.373	.380	.382	.383	.386
Jul	.353	.358	.364	.364	.372	.379	.381	.382	.385
Aug	.350	.355	.360	.360	.369	.376	.377	.378	.382
Sept	.340	.346	.351	.351	.359	.366	.368	.369	.372
Oct	.330	.335	.340	.340	.349	.356	.357	.358	.362
Nov	.319	.324	.329	.329	.338	.344	.346	.347	.350
Dec	.316	.321	.326	.326	.334	.341	.343	.343	.347
1990									
Jan	.308	.313	.318	.318	.326	.333	.335	.336	.339
Feb	.300	.305	.310	.310	.319	.325	.327	.328	.331
Mar	.287	.292	.297	.297	.306	.312	.314	.315	.318
Apr	.249	.254	.259	.259	.267	.273	.275	.276	.279
May	.239	.243	.248	.248	.256	.262	.264	.265	.268
Jun	.234	.238	.243	.243	.251	.257	.259	.260	.263
Jul	.233	.237	.242	.242	.250	.256	.258	.259	.262
Aug	.220	.225	.230	.230	.237	.244	.245	.246	.249
Sept	.209	.213	.218	.218	.226	.232	.234	.234	.237
Oct	.200	.204	.209	.209	.216	.223	.224	.225	.228
Nov	.202	.207	.212	.212	.219	.225	.227	.228	.231
Dec	.203	.208	.212	.212	.220	.226	.228	.229	.232
1991									
Jan	.200	.205	.210	.210	.217	.224	.225	.226	.229
Feb	.194	.199	.203	.203	.211	.217	.218	.219	.222
Mar	.189	.194	.199	.199	.206	.212	.214	.215	.218
Apr	.174	.179	.183	.183	.191	.197	.198	.199	.202
May	.171	.175	.180	.180	.187	.193	.195	.196	.199
Jun	.166	.170	.174	.174	.182	.188	.189	.190	.193
Jul	.168	.173	.177	.177	.185	.191	.192	.193	.196
Aug	.166	.170	.174	.174	.182	.188	.189	.190	.193
Sept	.161	.166	.170	.170	.178	.184	.185	.186	.189
Oct	.157	.161	.166	.166	.173	.179	.181	.181	.184
Nov	.153	.157	.162	.162	.169	.175	.176	.177	.180
Dec	.152	.156	.161	.161	.168	.174	.175	.176	.179
1992									
Jan	.153	.157	.162	.162	.169	.175	.176	.177	.180
Feb	.147	.151	.156	.156	.163	.169	.170	.171	.174
Mar	.143	.148	.152	.152	.159	.165	.167	.168	.170
Apr	.126	.130	.135	.135	.142	.148	.149	.150	.153
May	.122	.126	.131	.131	.138	.144	.145	.146	.149
Jun	.122	.126.	.131	.131	.138	.144	.145	.146	.149

Starting Month for Indexation	Apr	May	Jun	Jul	Aug	Sept	Oct	Nov	Dec
				Month of Disposal 1996					
Jul	.126	.130	.135	.135	.142	.148	.149	.150	.153
Aug	.125	.130	.134	.134	.141	.147	.148	.149	.152
Sept	.121	.126	.130	.130	.137	.143	.144	.145	.148
Oct	.117	.122	.126	.126	.133	.139	.140	.141	.144
Nov	.119	.123	.127	.127	.135	.140	.142	.142	.145
Dec	.123	.127	.131	.131	.139	.144	.146	.147	.149
1993									
Jan	.133	.138	.142	.142	.149	.155	.157	.157	.160
Feb	.126	.130	.135	.135	.142	.148	.149	.150	.153
Mar	.122	.126	.131	.131	.138	.144	.145	.146	.149
Apr	.112	.116	.120	.120	.127	.133	.134	.135	.138
May	.108	.112	.116	.116	.123	.129	.130	.131	.134
Jun	.109	.113	.117	.117	.124	.130	.131	.132	.135
Jul	.111	.115	.119	.119	.127	.132	.134	.134	.137
Aug	.106	.110	.115	.115	.122	.127	.129	.130	.132
Sept	.101	.106	.110	.110	.117	.123	.124	.125	.128
Oct	.102	.106	.111	.111	.118	.123	.125	.126	.128
Nov	.104	.108	.112	.112	.119	.125	.126	.127	.130
Dec	.101	.106	.110	.110	.117	.123	.124	.125	.128
1994									
Jan	.106	.110	.115	.115	.122	.127	.129	.130	.132
Feb	.100	.104	.108	.108	.115	.121	.122	.123	.126
Mar	.097	.101	.105	.105	.112	.118	.119	.120	.123
Apr	.084	.088	.092	.092	.099	.105	.106	.107	.110
May	.080	.084	.088	.088	.095	.101	.102	.103	.106
Jun	.080	.084	.088	.088	.095	.101	.102	.103	.106
Jul	.085	.090	.094	.094	.101	.106	.108	.108	.111
Aug	.080	.084	.088	.088	.095	.101	.102	.103	.106
Sept	.078	.082	.086	.086	.093	.099	.100	.101	.103
Oct	.076	.081	.085	.085	.092	.097	.098	.099	.102
Nov	.076	.080	.084	.084	.091	.096	.098	.098	.101
Dec	.071	.075	.079	.079	.086	.091	.092	.093	.096
1995									
Jan	.071	.075	.079	.079	.086	.091	.092	.093	.096
Feb	.064	.068	.072	.072	.079	.084	.086	.086	.089
Mar	.060	.064	.068	.068	.075	.080	.081	.082	.085
Apr	.049	.053	.057	.057	.064	.069	.070	.071	.074
May	.045	.049	.053	.053	.059	.065	.066	.067	.070
Jun	.043	.047	.051	.051	.058	.063	.065	.065	.058
Jul	.048	.052	.056	.056	.063	.068	.070	.070	.073
Aug	.043	.047	.051	.051	.057	.063	.064	.065	.067
Sept	.038	.042	.046	.046	.052	.058	.059	.060	.062
Oct	.043	.047	.051	.051	.058	.063	.065	.065	.068
Nov	.043	.047	.051	.051	.058	.063	.065	.065	.068
Dec	.037	.041	.045	.045	.052	.057	.058	.059	.062

Starting Month for Indexation	Apr	May	Jun	Jul	Aug	Sept	Oct	Nov	Dec
				Month of Disposal 1996					
1996									
Jan	.041	.045	.049	.049	.055	.061	.062	.063	.065
Feb	.036	.040	.044	.044	.050	.056	.057	.058	.060
Mar	.032	.036	.040	.040	.046	.051	.053	.053	.056
Apr	.024	.028	.032	.032	.039	.044	.045	.046	.048
May	.022	.026	.030	.030	.037	.042	.043	.044	.046
Jun	.022	.025	.029	.029	.036	.041	.042	.043	.046
Jul	.026	.030	.033	.033	.040	.045	.047	.047	.050
Aug	.021	.025	.029	.029	.035	.040	.042	.042	.045
Sept	.016	.020	.024	.024	.031	.036	.037	.038	.040
Oct	.016	.020	.024	.024	.031	.036	.037	.038	.040
Nov	.016	.019	.023	.023	.030	.035	.036	.037	.040
Dec	.012	.016	.020	.020	.027	.032	.033	.034	.036
1997									
Jan	.012	.016	.020	.020	.027	.032	.033	.034	.036
Feb	.008	.012	.016	.016	.023	.028	.029	.030	.032
Mar	.006	.010	.014	.014	.020	.025	.026	.027	.030
Apr		.004	.008	.008	.014	.019	.020	.021	.024
May			.004	.004	.010	.015	.017	.017	.020
Jun				.NIL	.006	.011	.013	.013	.016
Jul					.006	.011	.013	.013	.016
Aug						.005	.006	.007	.009
Sept							.001	.002	.004
Oct								.001	.003
Nov									.003

The Chancellor announced that all personal allowances and tax thresholds for 1998/99 will rise by approximately 3.6%, which is in line with inflation for the year to the end of September 1997.

Entitlement to the additional personal allowance is extended to women with children and incapacitated husbands living with them. This measure is backdated to 6 April 1997.

Looking ahead to 1999/2000, the rate of tax relief at which the married couple's allowance and related allowances is given will be reduced from 15% to 10%. Taxpayers aged 65 and over will be fully compensated for this reduction by receiving a corresponding increase, above indexation, in the age-related married couple's allowances.

1998/99 Personal Allowances

		£
Personal		4,195
Married couples		*1,900
Additional personal		*1,900
Age – personal	(age 65-74)	5,410
– married couples	(age 65-74)	*3,305
– personal	(age 75 and over)	5,600
– married couples	(age 75 and over)	*3,345
Income limit for age allowance		16,200
Widow's bereavement		*1,900
Relief for blind person (each)		1,330

* indicates allowances where tax relief is restricted to 15%

Tax Rates and Bands for 1998/99

Band of Taxable Income	Rate of Tax	Tax on Band	Cumulative Tax
£	%	£	£
0 – 4,300	20	860	860
4,301 – 27,100	23	5,244	6,104
over 27,100	40		

PAYE codes will change for the 1998/99 tax year as a result of the measures announced in the Budget. In general, taxpayers who only receive the personal allowance will have their code adjusted by their employer or pension provider. They will not receive a notice of coding from the Inland Revenue unless one is required for some other reason. Individuals who receive the married couple's allowance and related allowances will be sent an amended notice of coding. All amended codes will be operated on the first pay date after 17 May.

Rates of National Insurance Contributions for 1998/99
CLASS 1 Contributions for Employees

		Standard Rate		Contracted Out	
		On First £64.00	On Remainder	On First £64.00	On Remainder
Contributions levied on all weekly earnings if they reach	£64.00				
but do not exceed	£485.00	2%	10%	2%	8.4%
If weekly earnings exceed	£485.00	No additional contributions		No additional contributions	

Reduced Rate for Married Women and Widows with a Valid Election Certificate		3.85%
Men over 65 and Women over 60		Nil
Lower Earnings Limit	• Weekly	£64.00
	• Monthly	£278.00
	• Annually	£3,328.00
Upper Earnings Limit	• Weekly	£485.00
	• Monthly	£2,102.00
	• Annually	£25,220.00

CLASS 2 Contributions for the Self-Employed

Weekly flat rate	£6.35
Small earnings exception	£3,590.00

CLASS 3 Voluntary Contributions

Weekly rate	£6.25

CLASS 4 Contributions for the Self-Employed — 6% of profits between £7,310 and £25,220

National Insurance Reforms
The following proposals are to take effect from April 1999:

Employees – No liability on earnings up to the single person's tax allowance. Earnings above that level up to the upper earnings limit (currently £485 per week) will be chargeable at 10% (8.4% for contracted out employees).

Self-Employed – Proposals still under consideration.

Working Families Tax Credit
This scheme is to replace the existing Family Credit in October 1999. It is designed to provide a guaranteed minimum income for working families over and above the minimum wage and will incorporate a new childcare tax credit which will be worth 70% of eligible childcare costs up to a ceiling on costs of £100 per week for one child and £150 for two or more children. The scheme will be administered by the Inland Revenue and from April 2000 will be payable through the employee's wage packet. The self-employed will receive the credit direct from the Inland Revenue.

The essential requirement is for the family to have children and for at least one of the parents to work 16 or more hours per week. The credit contains the following elements in addition to the Childcare Tax Credit referred to above:

		£ per week, 1998/99 prices
Basic tax credit (one per family)		48.80
Tax credits for each child aged	0-10	14.85
each child aged	11-15	20.45
each child aged	16-18	25.40
Extra tax credit for working		10.80
30 hours or more a week		

The full credit is payable if the family's net income is less than £90 per week. Above this threshold the credit is reduced by 55p for every extra £1 of net income.

Relief for Maintenance Payments

Tax relief on maintenance payments is linked to the level of the married couple's allowance. It follows that the amount of maintenance payments attracting tax relief at 15% for 1998/99 goes up to £1,900. Similarly, relief on these payments will be reduced to 10% from 6 April 1999.

Income Tax on Savings

No changes are proposed to the tax charge on income from savings, such as bank and building society interest, which is now 20%. Higher-rate taxpayers will continue to pay tax on this type of income at 40%.

Mortgage Interest Relief

The overall limit on borrowings for the purchase of the borrower's home up to which the interest is eligible for tax relief is unchanged at £30,000. As already announced, the rate of tax relief on mortgage interest reduces from 15% to 10% from 6 April 1998. Nevertheless, tax relief at the basic rate will continue to be given on interest on certain loans taken out by individuals over 65 to purchase life annuities.

Pension Schemes Earnings Limit

Pension contributions for members of occupational pension schemes established on or after 14 March 1989, and for members joining schemes established before that date on or after 1 June 1989, are restricted to those based on a maximum annual earnings limit. This earnings cap is increased from £84,000 to £87,600 from 6 April 1998. It also applies to all personal pension schemes.

'Millennium Gift Aid'

The minimum donation limit under Gift Aid is reduced from £250 to £100 where an individual gives to causes which support education and anti-poverty projects in the world's poorest countries. Furthermore, individuals who make a number of smaller donations by instalments totalling £100, will also be entitled to relief.

'Millennium Gift Aid' is to be launched later this year and will continue until the end of the year 2000.

Company Cars and Car Fuel

In an attempt to reduce the impact on the environment of emissions from company cars, the Chancellor is intending to discourage employers from providing, and employees from accepting, free fuel so that more company car drivers face the full cost of the fuel they use for private motoring. It is proposed that:

- Scale charges for petrol provided for private motoring in company cars will increase by 20% over and above the usual increases in line with pump prices, including fuel duty, in 1998/99. Similar increases will take place for the years 1999/2000 to 2002/03.

- Scale charges for diesel provided for private motoring will increase further to align them with those for petrol cars of the same engine capacity.

- From 6 April 1999 the extra cost of enabling company cars to run on cleaner and greener road fuel gases, when calculating the tax charge on company cars, will be disregarded.

- Consideration will be given to proposals to replace existing business mileage discounts with discounts for driving fewer private miles in company cars.

The rates of Car Fuel Benefit for 1998/99 are as follows:

	Engine Size cc	Fuel Benefit £
Petrol	0 – 1400	1 010
	1401 – 2000	1,280
	over 2000	1,890
Diesel	0 – 2000	1,280
	over 2000	1,890
Cars without a cylinder capacity		1,890

Employee Travel and Subsistence

From 6 April 1998 the new provisions dealing with the taxation of employees' business travel and subsistence expenses come into force. These changes, which are intended to make the rules both fairer and simpler, were originally announced in the November 1996 Budget Statement.

Starting with the 1998/99 tax year an employee, who makes a qualifying business journey, will be entitled to tax relief on the full cost of the trip. The full cost includes both travelling expenses and any subsistence directly associated with the journey such as an evening meal and accommodation for an overnight stay. The new rules will be of particular significance to:

- Site-based workers. Travel and subsistence expenses are only free of tax if an employee is actually at a site for less than two years.

- Employees with areas. All travel by an employee within the area is not taxable.

- Employees with more than one permanent place of work who will find that travelling and subsistence expenses associated with either workplace will not be allowable.

Foreign Earnings Deduction

To counter exploitation of the existing rules, it is proposed with immediate effect to end the general Foreign Earnings Deduction, except for seafarers. The Foreign Earnings Deduction provided 100% deduction for earnings from employment carried out wholly or partly abroad during a qualifying period of 365 days or more. The income was thus free of UK tax and possibly overseas tax as well. With careful tax planning no tax could be paid at all on these earnings.

Employment Termination Settlements

It has become common for employment termination settlements to provide for some benefits to continue after termination. Under existing rules there can be problems in taxing benefits-in-kind provided by a former employer in such circumstances. The charge to tax, which must be made in full at the time the employment is terminated, is on the value of the right to future benefits. These may be difficult to value since the timespans on which they depend, such as until death or finding a new job, are not easy to predict.

Furthermore, payments and benefits, whenever received or enjoyed, must be taxed as income in the year of termination. This often means that an individual's tax liability for that year has to be revised on several occasions. This sort of situation does not fit in neatly with Self Assessment for individual taxpayers.

In order to address these issues the 1998 Finance Bill will include a new basis for taxing such benefits and payments only to the extent they arise and in the year in which they are received or enjoyed – rather than being treated as income of the year of termination.

The £30,000 redundancy exemption is unaffected by these modifications.

Individual Savings Accounts

The Chancellor has obviously taken on board comments made about the Government's proposals for a new, instant-access, tax-free savings account which was the subject of a consultative document issued in December 1997. The arrangement for savers holding Personal Equity Plans and Tax Exempt Special Savings Accounts, as well as the main features of the new Individual Savings Accounts, are:

Personal Equity Plans (PEPs)

- Savers with PEPs at 5 April 1999 will be allowed to continue holding them under the existing rules and outside the new savings account.
- For the first five years, until 5 April 2004, a 10% tax credit will be paid on dividends from UK equities.
- The amount that can be subscribed to the new savings account will be unaffected by the value of PEP holdings.
- No subscriptions to PEPs may be made after 5 April 1999.

Tax Exempt Special Savings Accounts (TESSAs)

- TESSAs taken out by 5 April 1999 will be able to run their full five-year course.

- Savers will be able to continue subscribing to such TESSAs under existing rules.

- When the TESSA matures they will be able to transfer their capital (but not accumulated interest) into the cash component of the new savings account.

- The amount that can be subscribed to the new account will not be affected by annual TESSA subscriptions nor any capital transferred from a TESSA.

- No new TESSAs can be taken out after 5 April 1999.

Individual Savings Accounts

Individuals, who are both resident and ordinarily resident in the UK for tax purposes and are aged 18 and over, will be eligible to subscribe to the new account. It will start on 6 April 1999 and be guaranteed to run for at least ten years. It will be reviewed after seven years to decide on any changes after the initial ten-year period. The Individual Savings Account can include three components:

- Cash (including National Savings)

- Life assurance; and

- Stocks and shares.

In the first year of the scheme only (1999/2000) the annual subscription limit will be £7,000, of which no more than £3,000 can go into cash and £1,000 into life assurance. In subsequent years the annual subscription limit will be £5,000, of which no more than £1,000 can go into cash and £1,000 into life insurance. There will be no lifetime investment limit and the account will be completely free of tax. In addition, a 10% tax credit will be paid for the first five years of the scheme, that is until 5 April 2004, on dividends from UK equities. There will be no statutory lock-in period or minimum subscription.

Savers will have a choice of managers; each year there will be two options. The first option is that they can go to a single manager who must offer an account which can accept the overall subscription. This means that the account must include the stocks and shares component, but does not need to offer either of the other two components (cash and life insurance). Savers will be able to subscribe up to £5,000 (£7,000 in 1999/2000) to the stocks and shares component. If, in addition, the manager offers the cash or life insurance components savers will be able to subscribe up to £1,000 (£3,000 in 1999/2000) to the cash component and £1,000 to the life insurance component, with the balance going into stocks and shares.

The second option is that savers can go to separate managers – one for each component – and subscribe up to £3,000 in stocks and shares, £1,000 (£3,000 in 1999/2000) to cash and £1,000 to life insurance. These fixed individual limits will help to ensure that the overall annual limit can be satisfactorily monitored.

Shares acquired under a public offer, or received when a building society or mutual insurer demutualises, cannot be transferred into the new savings account.

The Government has decided against proceeding with the idea of a prize draw.

Venture Capital

The Chancellor announced proposals for more generous and better targeted incentives to promote investment and enterprise. The Enterprise Investment Scheme and Capital Gains Tax reinvestment relief are to be rationalised to create a unified scheme, taking effect from 6 April 1998. For investors, the main features of the scheme are:

- An increase of 50% to £150,000 per annum in the amount an individual can invest in eligible shares with the benefit of Income Tax relief, at the fixed rate of 20%, and exemption from Capital Gains Tax on gains made after five years;

- Unlimited deferral relief from Capital Gains Tax for individuals (whether or not they qualify for Income Tax relief) and trustees where chargeable gains on disposals are invested in eligible shares;

- An increase from £15,000 to £25,000 in the amount an individual may invest in shares issued in the first half of a tax year, and qualify for Income Tax relief for the previous year.

The Accrued Income Scheme

The operation of the Accrued Income Scheme ensures that when an interest-bearing security is transferred, both buyer and seller are only taxed on the proportion of the interest relating to their respective periods of ownership. At present there is an anomaly for basic- and lower-rate taxpayers. The charge is set at the basic rate of 23% but relief may be either at the basic rate or the lower rate of 20%. From 6 April 1998 charges will be made, and relief given, at the lower rate of 20% for both basic- and lower-rate taxpayers. As now, higher-rate taxpayers and trustees will continue to be chargeable at the higher rate, or at the rate applicable to trusts, as appropriate.

Taxation of Life Insurance Policy Holders

Gains made by those who hold certain life insurance policies are chargeable to tax when chargeable events occur, such as:

- The maturity of a policy; or

- When there is a surrender or sale of some or all of the rights under the policy.

However, if a policy is held in trust, the gain generally falls on the settlor. No liability arises if the settlor is dead or not resident in the United Kingdom. It is proposed to remove this anomaly. The trustees will become liable to pay the tax if they are resident in the United Kingdom. If they are not resident the charge may fall on a UK beneficiary under the trust to the extent that he or she receives benefits from the trust funds. The new rules will apply to chargeable events on or after 6 April 1998.

A 'personal portfolio bond' is a type of insurance policy designed primarily for tax-avoidance purposes. It is usually held with a non-UK insurer. The benefits under such a policy are, or may be linked to, a portfolio of assets that is personal to the policy holder. Because the holder can decide when to surrender the policy, he or she is able to defer for many years the tax charge on any income or gain arising on the investments held in the policy. It is even possible for the policy holder to arrange to be a non-resident when the policy comes to an end, and so escape paying tax altogether.

Under the Budget proposals there will be an additional tax charge on a deemed 'gain' equal to 15% of the sum of the total premiums paid up to the end of each 'policy year' and the total of deemed 'gains' from previous years. The charge on the deemed 'gain' will be in addition to the normal tax charge which would arise on a chargeable event.

The additional tax charge will not be imposed in any policy year which ends before 6 April 1999, thus giving those who have purchased these types of bond the opportunity to surrender them before the proposed annual charge arises.

Capital Allowances

Expenditure on plant and machinery by small- and medium-sized businesses in the twelve months to 1 July 1999 will attract a 40% first-year allowance. This compares to a 50% rate of allowance on expenditure incurred in the year to the beginning of July 1998.

Value Added Tax

From the start of their next accounting period after 6 April 1998, businesses must use the new quarterly scale charges for motor fuel as shown in the following table:

	Diesel		Petrol	
Car	Scale Charge	VAT	Scale Charge	VAT
cc	£	£	£	£
1400 or less	196	29.19	212	31.57
1401 – 2000	196	29.19	268	39.91
Over 2000	248	36.93	396	58.97

Capital Gains Tax

The Capital Gains Tax annual exemption limit is increased to £6,800.

A number of fundamental changes to the structure of Capital Gains Tax are proposed which will take effect from 6 April 1998. The proposals will:

- Withdraw indexation for periods after 5 April 1998.

- Reduce the amount of chargeable gain according to the period for which the asset has been held, with a greater reduction for business assets than for others.

- Phase out retirement relief over a five-year period.

Indexation is to be replaced by a taper. Accordingly, for gains realised on or after 6 April 1998 the indexation allowance will be given for periods to 5 April 1998, but not thereafter.

The taper will reduce the amount of chargeable gain according to how long the asset has been held for periods after 5 April 1998. The taper will be more generous for business assets than for non-business assets. It will be applied to the net gains that are chargeable after the deduction of any losses that are suffered in the same tax year and of any losses that are carried forward from earlier years. The annual exemption will then be deducted from the tapered gains. The allocation of losses to gains for this purpose will be on the basis that produces the lowest tax charge.

The taper will substantially reduce the Capital Gains Tax charge on the disposal of long-held business assets. Retirement relief will therefore be phased out from 6 April 1999 by a gradual reduction of the relief thresholds. The relief will cease to be available from 6 April 2003.

Acquisitions of shares and other securities are presently 'pooled'. The introduction of the taper means that pooling will have to cease for acquisitions on or after 6 April 1998. This is necessary since the date of each acquisition will need to be recorded and retained. New rules for identifying shares disposed of will apply. Disposals after 5 April 1998 will be identified with acquisitions in the following order:

- Same-day acquisitions (under the existing rule).
- Acquisitions within the following thirty days (see bed and breakfasting below).
- Previous acquisitions after 5 April 1998, identifying the most recent acquisitions first.
- Any shares comprised in the pool at 5 April 1998.
- Any shares held at 5 April 1982.
- Any shares acquired before 6 April 1965.

If the above identification rules fail to exhaust the shares disposed of, they are to be identified with subsequent acquisitions.

Bed and breakfasting (i.e. selling shares and buying them back shortly afterwards in order to reduce the Capital Gains Tax bill) will no longer have the desired tax consequences. For Capital Gains Tax purposes, any shares sold and repurchased within a thirty-day period will be matched, so that the gain or loss which would have otherwise arisen by reference to shares already held will not be realised. This new thirty-day rule is to operate with effect from Budget Day.

Individuals who have acquired assets before they leave the United Kingdom for a period of residence abroad of less than five complete tax years will remain chargeable to Capital Gains Tax on gains made on those assets while abroad. The new rules will apply to individuals who leave the United Kingdom for tax residence abroad on or after Budget Day.

Inheritance Tax

From 6 April 1998 the nil-rate band increases from £215,000 to £223,000.